# CyberSurfer

# The OWL Internet Guide for Kids

## Nyla Ahmad
**Editor, OWL Magazine**

*Directory researched and written by*

## Keltie Thomas
Managing Editor, OWL Magazine

*Illustrations by*

## Martha Newbigging

# Owl Books

Owl Books are published by Greey de Pencier Books Inc., 179 John Street, Suite 500, Toronto, Ontario M5T 3G5

OWL and the Owl colophon are trademarks of Owl Communications.
Greey de Pencier Books Inc. is a licensed user of trademarks of Owl Communications.

Text, disk contents, and directory compilation © 1996 Owl Books
Illustrations for book and disk © 1996 Martha Newbigging
Photo illustration of CyberSurfer © 1996 Bob Anderson

Disk developed and programmed by AVM OnLine

Distributed in the United States by Firefly Books (U.S.) Inc.,
230 Fifth Avenue, Suite 1607, New York, NY 10001.

This book was published with the generous support of the Canada Council,
the Ontario Arts Council and the Ontario Publishing Centre.

**Canadian Cataloguing in Publication Data**

Ahmad, Nyla.
       CyberSurfer: the OWL Internet guide for kids

Accompanied by 1 computer disk for Windows and Mac.
Includes index.
ISBN 1-895688-50-7

1. Internet (Computer network) — Juvenile literature.
I. Newbigging, Martha.  II. Title

TK5105.875.I57A55 1996     j004.6'7        C95-932251-5

**Author Dedication**

To my network of providers: my parents for their endless support, my brothers for their "smileys,"
Rob for his content, and the Sandlers for answering all my FAQs.

**Acknowledgements**

The author thanks Sheba "Gopher-it!" Meland, Keltie "Surf-and-Seek" Thomas, Kat "FAQ" Mototsune,
Julia "GIF" Naimska, Martha "Newbie" Newbigging, Kathrine "Router" Pummell, Andrea "Knowbot" McGrory,
and of course, Ben Nelson, Ben's parents, and PJ.
The publishers would like to express their appreciation to Andrea McGrory,
for cheerfully working miracles and dispensing wise advice through it all.
We also acknowledge the assistance of Netaccess Inc. of Hamilton, Ontario.

**Project Consultants**

Peter-John Maxwell  Internet and Information Technology Consultant

Andrea McGrory     Project Coordinator, Ontario Education Highway, Ontario Ministry of Education

John Nelson         Section Manager, Access Network, Bell Canada
                     Director, Hamilton-Wentworth FreeNet

Peter Skillen        Program Leader, Computers in Education, North York Board of Education

**Photo Credits**

Cover: wave, Jason Childs/Masterfile; hand, Tony Arruza; surfer, Bob Anderson. Pages 9: Skyline Displays; 17 left, Northern Telecom;
right, Comstock/Comstock; 19, Renee Knoeber; 28, Nick Carter/Orangutan Reintroduction Project; 29 top, Superstock/P.R. Productions;
bottom, Ability OnLine; 35, J. Ridgway Photography; 42, Douglas Mason/EarthTreks; 43 top, NASA; bottom, Dream Weaver;
50 top, Robert Willet/News Observer/Sygma; bottom, Jim Bounds/Raleigh News Observer/Sygma.

Design & Art Direction: Julia Naimska
Cover Photo Illustration: Bob Anderson

Printed in Canada

A    B    C    D    E    F

# Contents

# Get Set for the Net!

You are entering a new world — a world of passwords, e-mail, hackers, lurkers, and cyberpals. Here you can log on, chat with millions of people around the world, surf, visit NASA, run with a Gopher, or do your homework with Archie. To get here you just fire up your **computer\***, head for the high-tech Information Superhighway, and get onto the Net. Does any of this make sense to you? Probably not — so read on!

The Internet, or "Net" for short, is a world-wide **network** of computer networks. What's that? Think of a spider spinning its web. First the spider spins a few strands of silk joined in diamond-shaped sections. As the web grows, the sections are attached to more sections. On and on spider goes, building more sections and attaching them to the rest until, finally, the web is complete. The Internet is like a spider's web except that, instead of silk, the Internet "weaves" telephone lines to create sections of linked computers. Computer experts began creating the Internet by linking a few computers together to form a group, or network. Then they linked, or hooked up, this first network to other networks with cables, microwaves, **satellites**, and the other high-tech systems that carry electronic information around the world.

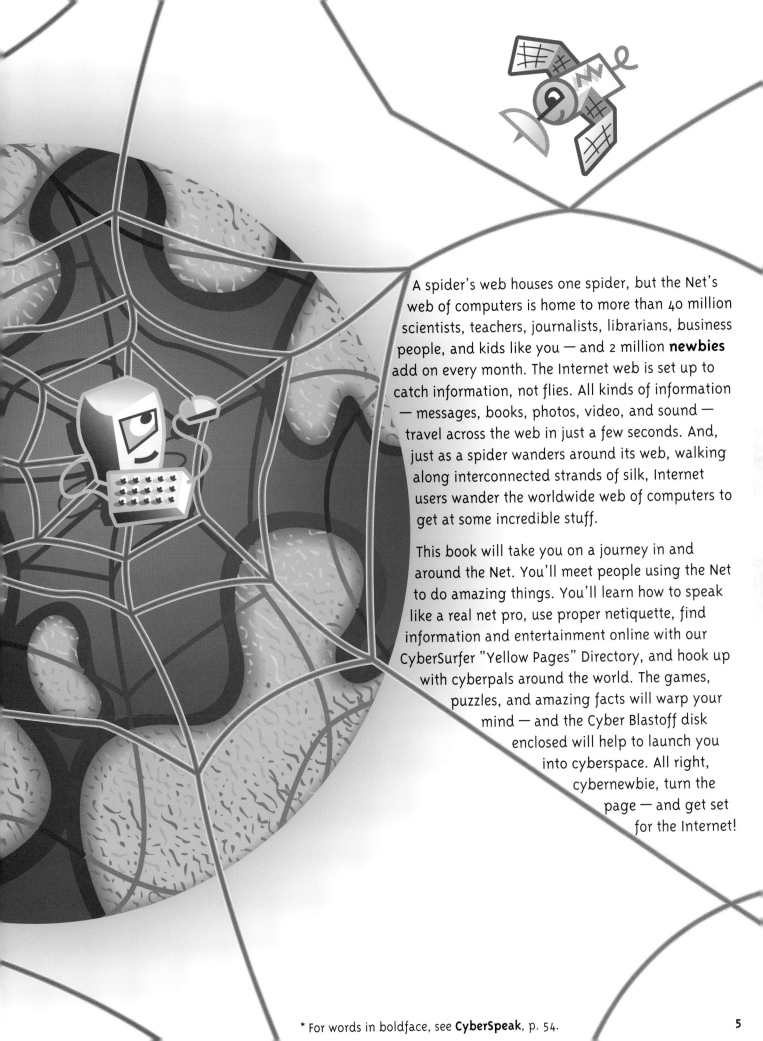

A spider's web houses one spider, but the Net's web of computers is home to more than 40 million scientists, teachers, journalists, librarians, business people, and kids like you — and 2 million **newbies** add on every month. The Internet web is set up to catch information, not flies. All kinds of information — messages, books, photos, video, and sound — travel across the web in just a few seconds. And, just as a spider wanders around its web, walking along interconnected strands of silk, Internet users wander the worldwide web of computers to get at some incredible stuff.

This book will take you on a journey in and around the Net. You'll meet people using the Net to do amazing things. You'll learn how to speak like a real net pro, use proper netiquette, find information and entertainment online with our CyberSurfer "Yellow Pages" Directory, and hook up with cyberpals around the world. The games, puzzles, and amazing facts will warp your mind — and the Cyber Blastoff disk enclosed will help to launch you into cyberspace. All right, cybernewbie, turn the page — and get set for the Internet!

# History of a Hooked-Up World

The **Internet** is today's newest and fastest way to communicate with people around the world. But you know what? The technology that makes the Net possible isn't really new. Some brilliant thinkers throughout techno-history invented the telephones, radios, computers, and other stuff that the Internet needs to operate — and some were invented more than 150 years ago! Take a look at this timeline of communication history to find out who the geniuses were and how their brainwaves affect us today.

| 1844 | 1858 | 1867 |
|---|---|---|
| Morse invents the telegraph and sends the first electronic message. | First transatlantic cable is laid, allowing intercontinental electric communication. | The first typewriter is invented. Things no longer need to be written by hand. |

## Electronic Messages

Samuel Morse invented the telegraph in 1844. For the first time, words could travel rapidly over long distances, wherever telegraph wires could be strung. When its "key" was pressed, the telegraph transmitted an electric pulse over wires to another telegraph machine. Each pulse made a "dot" or a "dash" on a strip of paper in the receiving telegraph. These dots and dashes were called Morse Code, and were translated into the letters of the alphabet. More than 100 years after the invention of the telegraph, the first computer was invented. The computer also transmits a code of pulses. But it does the code-to-letter translation automatically, and also has a "memory" where it can store data. You can still print a copy on paper, but only if you want to.

## Going the Distance

Once messages could be transmitted instead of mailed, they could be sent farther and faster. A transatlantic cable beneath the Atlantic Ocean, between North America and Europe, was the start of intercontinental electric communication. The cable carried telegraph signals across the Atlantic in just minutes — instead of the three months a postal ship would take to carry letters the same distance. Nearly 100 years later, people started to send messages around the globe through the air instead of under the ocean — with satellites. A **satellite dish** can send electronic signals up to a satellite orbiting 36,000 km (22,320 mi) above us in space. Space satellites then reflect, or bounce, these signals back down to Earth to other dishes around the globe — all within seconds.

## The Keys of Progress

Before the first typewriter was invented, everything that wasn't printed on a press had to be written out by hand. People spent weeks handwriting pages of text to be printed in newspapers, books, and other important documents. In 1867, a newspaper editor named Christopher Sholes invented the first fast and efficient way to put text on paper. He called it the typewriter. The "keys of letters" he invented got the whole world "typing." Nearly 100 years after the first typewriter, the first computer network was created. With networked computers, a user can type a message onto the keyboard of one computer and have it appear on the screen of another computer. Typed messages can be sent instantly — without the use of a single piece of paper!

| 1946 | 1957 | 1960 |
|---|---|---|
| The Electronic Numerical Integrator and Calculator (ENIAC) begins to operate. | First satellite sends information back from space. | Scientists develop the first computer network to transmit messages electronically. |

## 1876

Bell invents the telephone. It sends the human voice over electronic wires.

## 1889

Edison's phonograph and Eastman's flexible photographic film are introduced.

## 1894

Marconi develops the radio. It sends signals through the air without using wires.

# Bells and Whistles

One invention really changed the way we communicate with each other, and we use it every day — it's the telephone. Alexander Graham Bell, perhaps one of the greatest inventors ever, created his first telephone back in 1876. For the first time, people could actually talk to someone far away. Today, more than 525,000,000 telephones ring throughout the world, and more than 400 billion telephone conversations take place each year. The telephone lines that transmit voice messages from coast to coast are also the backbone of the Internet. Less than 100 years had passed after Bell's first telephone conversation when the Internet was created to get computers "talking" to each other over telephone lines, no matter how far away or remote they might be.

# Hear It, See It

Around 1889, two major inventions took place in sound and pictures. Thomas A. Edison, inventor of the light bulb, created the phonograph, a machine that could record and play sound. George Eastman, founder of Eastman-Kodak Co., created a photographic film that made way for the technology of modern cameras. As time went on, these two technologies began working together and advancing, so people could better hear and see what they recorded. By the turn of the century, motion pictures were invented, and television followed a few decades afterwards. Within 100 years of the first major breakthroughs in pictures and sound, we were living in an audiovisual world. Today, audio and video data can be transmitted from one computer to another.

# A Wireless World

Guglielmo Marconi developed the radio back in 1894. It must have seemed like magic, as invisible signals travelled through the air from one radio antenna to another, allowing first the Morse Code and then voices to be heard loud and clear. This set the wireless world in motion! Today, a concert performer sings into a wireless microphone. Wireless microphones, and many other everyday devices, work with radio waves. Scientists say that by the year 2000, just over 100 years after Marconi's first radio, a new wireless world may exist. The possibilities seem endless — video-conferencing, remote surgery, and virtual reality. We'll be able to get in touch with anyone, from anywhere in the world, without the need of a single plug, cable, or power socket.

## 1969

The Internet starts sending messages between computers around the world.

## 1994

Video and audio are transmitted over the Internet.

## 2000

Experts predict a fully interactive system of communication, online and wireless.

## Reality Byte

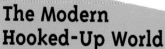

In the 1970s, the U.S. Defense Department began looking into computer networks. They realized that, for computers to understand each other, a network needed a standard "language." So they developed a language, called the Internet Protocol (IP). This made it possible for computers to chat it up on the Net.

## The Modern Hooked-Up World

What do light, pigeons, drums, smoke, and the Internet have in common? Communication. They're all ways that have been used to send signals or messages across a distance. Humans have tried to communicate over long distances for thousands of years, and the gadgets and gizmos used to send messages near or far have changed a lot. Today's communication technology builds on all that came before. Communication experts are always finding new and better ways to send messages farther and faster around the globe. Why? People want to be in touch with others because the more in touch we are, the more we can learn from each other. And the more we learn, the more we all know.

## FAMOUS FIRST WORDS

"WOW! It actually works!" That's what a scientist might have been thinking the first time an invention finally worked, but that's not what most of them said. Here are the first messages transmitted on breakthroughs in communications. Can you identify who sent what? (Answers on page 56.)

1. "What hath God wrought!"

2. "Europe and America are united by telegraphy. Glory to God in the highest, on Earth peace, and good will toward men."

3. "Mr. Watson, come here. I want you."

4. "Good morning, Mr. Edison. Glad to see you back. I hope you are satisfied with the kineto-phonograph."

5. "S"

A. Sent by Thomas Edison's assistant

B. Sent by Alexander Graham Bell

C. First message to Marconi over the radio

D. Sent by Samuel Morse

E. First transatlantic message

# CYBERSTORY

## Building a New World

On April 21, 1995, more than a thousand kids got together to "build a new world" in honor of Earth Day. Their world was a globe five storeys tall and wider than two buses parked end-to-end. It was made up of 1620 plastic panels, 5000 bolts, 812 hub pieces, 568 litres (150 gal) of paint, and 2700 kg (6000 lbs) of steel — it took 9000 kg (20,000 lbs) of sand just to keep it from tumbling over! But before the kids could actually build a planet modeled on Earth, they had to learn about our world. Students involved in the Building a New World project spent months studying the real world on the Internet, using maps, satellite images, weather systems, and earth studies. They participated in discussions with international experts. Using information and resources from all over the world, the kids investigated the different parts of our planet and tried to figure out what makes it work. And then they used what they learned to build their own.

*Math, science, and engineering can be fun. Kids met on the Net to research the Earth and to design a world of their own.*

*The project had big results — a perfect replica of Earth, exactly one-millionth the size of our world.*

# Life Is a Highway

Start your computer engine, put your mouse to the metal, and get ready to roll down the fastest highway in the world — one that'll get you from St. John's to Seattle to Singapore in just a few seconds! The Information Superhighway, or I-Way for short, is what many people call the Internet and its web of computer communication. And, you know, that's a great name for it.

Take a look at a highway map of your country. You'll find a network of roads linking all the cities and towns to each other. Pick two destinations on your map (the further they are from each other the better) and see how many different ways — short or long, using big roads or small — you can find. Too many routes to count, right?

In many ways the Internet is like your highway map. The Net is home to computers instead of the towns and cities on your map. Telephone connections through wire, radio, or satellite "routes" are the highways and roads you travel to visit those distant locations. Just imagine how many millions of ways, long or short, you can take to get from a computer in St. John's to another in Singapore.

The good news for you is that you don't need a license to drive on the I-Way. All you need is a computer, a modem, the right software, a host, and a telephone line. With these things, you can get online and blast off into cyberspace. Read on, and you'll find out all you need to know about gearing up, hooking up, and life on the I-Way!

## Where Is Cyberspace?

Cyberspace is the high-tech zone that exists behind the flickering light of your computer screen, in the wires of your telephone line, and up in space between orbiting satellites. It's the "place" where digital bits of information — from your computer and from the 40 million others on the Net — meet. It's not a physical place where you can go, like a city or park, but it's a place your computer can take you to. The term "cyberspace" was first used back in 1984 by author William Gibson in his sci-fi novel *Neuromancer*. Today, cyberspace is how most people describe the world of the Net. Just think of a telephone conversation — where do those chats really take place? They happen in the phone line that connects you and your pal. On the same digital map of the electronic universe, the computers on the Net chat it up in the far reaches of cyberspace!

# Life on the I-Way

Take a trip down the **I-Way** and you'll find yourself zipping across phone lines, crossing over bridges, bouncing off of satellites, and flying across the world within seconds. To make it all happen, computer scientists and other experts use the latest in high-tech tools to create the fastest I-Way on Earth. Here's how it works.

## Road Map of Cyberspace

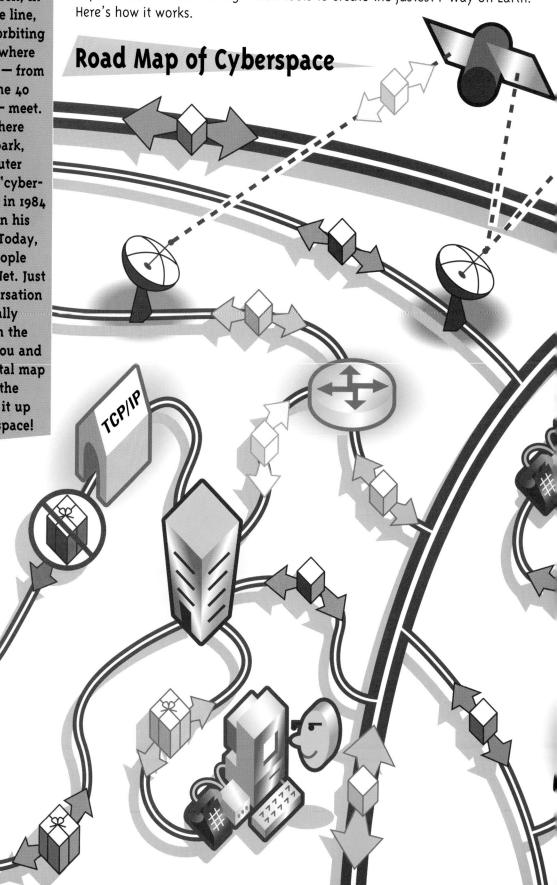

TCP/IP

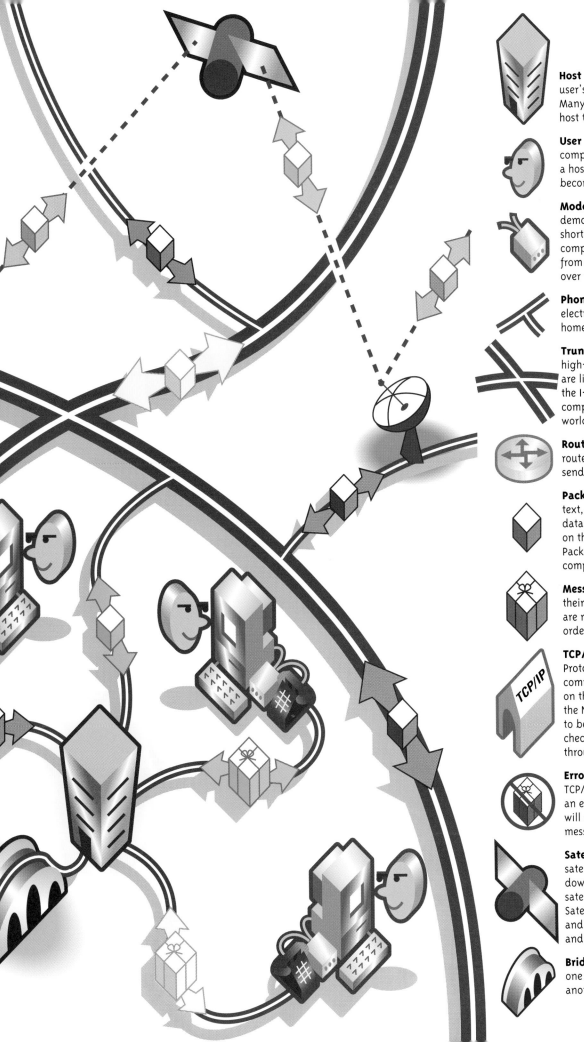

**Host** A host computer links a user's computer to the Internet. Many people can use the same host to get to the Net.

**User** To get on the I-Way, your computer must be connected to a host computer. Then you become a Net user.

**Modem** Your modulator-demodulator, or modem for short, sends signals from your computer and receives signals from other computers on the Net over phone lines.

**Phone Lines** Information travels electronically in and out of your home through telephone cables.

**Trunk Lines** Long-distance, high-speed digital connections are like the main highways of the I-Way. They link the phone companies working around the world together on the Net.

**Routers** Like a post office, routers choose the best route to send your message.

**Packets** Messages — digital text, pictures, or audio or video data — are broken up and travel on the Net in tiny packets. Packets travel between your computer and others on the Net.

**Messages** Once they've reached their destination, tiny packets are reassembled in their correct order to be read as a message.

**TCP/IP** Transmission Control Protocol/Internet Protocol is the communication standard used on the Net. All information on the Net must meet this protocol to be transmitted. Packets are checked for correct protocol throughout the Net.

**Error** Packets that do not meet TCP/IP are sent back to you as an error. Your computer screen will show a message that the message wasn't sent.

**Satellites** Signals zip up to a satellite in space and then are downlinked, or reflected, to a satellite dish back on Earth. Satellites make it easy to send and receive information quickly and smoothly around the globe.

**Bridges** A bridge lets a user in one network "crossover" to another network on the Net.

# Driving Lessons

Ready for a few road tips? Getting **online** and hopping onto the computer I-Way isn't difficult, but there are a few things you should learn and some equipment you'll need. Here's a quick lesson on driving into cyberspace.

## Your Computer Vehicle

In many ways your computer terminal is like a car. It's the vehicle that can take you where you need to go. A computer is basically a machine that can store information, accept instructions, and then take action. The world's first computer was 24 m (80 ft) long, 3 m (10 ft) high, and weighed more than 27 tonnes (30 tons). Today computers are small enough to fit on your desk, on your lap, or even around your wrist. Just as there are many different types of cars — some are faster, sportier, or sleeker than others — there are many types of computers. But the type of computer you take for a drive down the I-Way doesn't really matter. The important thing is that it works. And just like a car, a computer is useless without a driver — that's you!

## The Driver's Seat

Sitting in front of your computer terminal is just like being in the driver's seat. You are the person in control. You steer through the I-Way by pressing keys on your keyboard or by clicking with your mouse. Your keyboard is connected to your computer's central processing unit, or **CPU** for short, and this is where your steering power comes from. Beneath the keys on your keyboard is a circuit board that transmits the commands you press through the keys into a digital code (see *Digital vs. Analog* on opposite page) that your computer understands. Your mouse is also connected to your keyboard and CPU, and it talks to your computer in electronic digital computer codes, too. Together, the keyboard and mouse are your **input devices**, letting you command your computer.

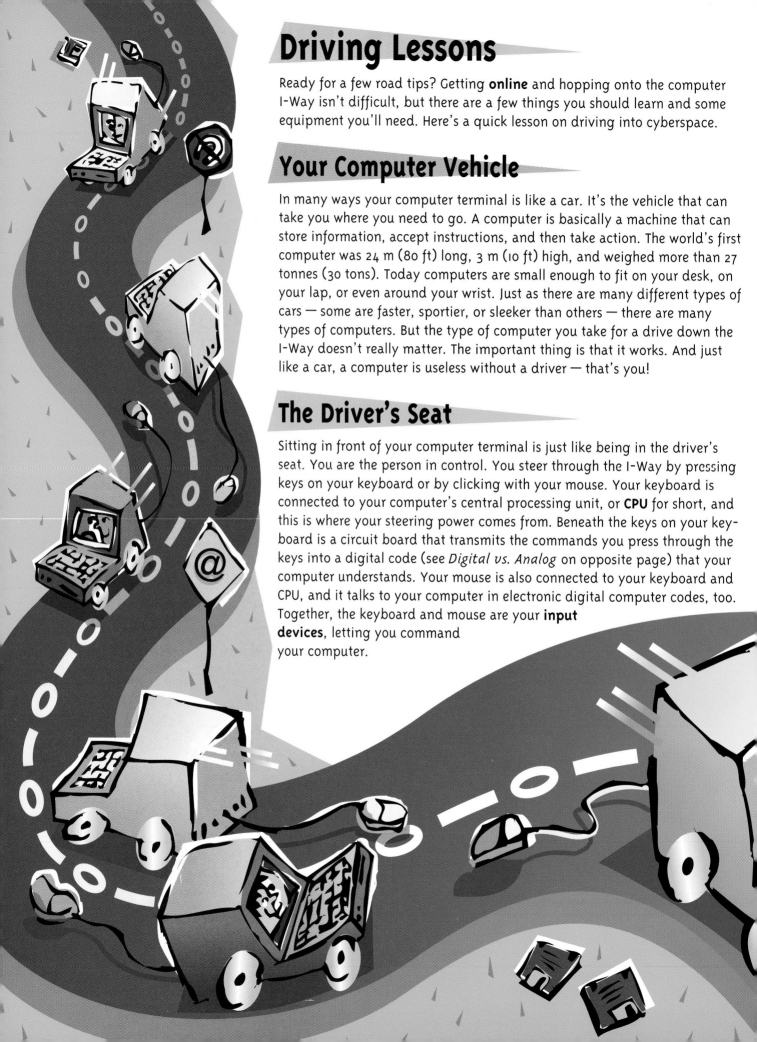

# A Modem-Powered Engine

Your **modem** is the engine that powers your computer vehicle and lets you cruise around the I-Way. A modem is like an automatic translator. It takes **digital** signals from your CPU and translates them into **analog** signals ready to travel through phone lines to other computers. It also takes the analog signals that come in from the phone lines and other computers, and translates them into digital signals that your CPU understands. Without a modem, your computer is just a computer. But with a modem and some kind of Internet access, your computer is a high-powered vehicle that can blast you into cyberspace!

## BINARY BABBLE

Be a digital detective. Grab a piece of paper and use the binary code below to figure what the babble on the right is all about. (Answer on page 56.)

| | | | | | | | |
|---|---|---|---|---|---|---|---|
| A | 00001 | N | 01110 | 00111 | | 00101 | 11011 |
| B | 00010 | O | 01111 | | | | |
| C | 00011 | P | 10000 | | | | |
| D | 00100 | Q | 11110 | 11100 | | 00101 | 11011 |
| E | 00101 | R | 11101 | | | | |
| F | 00110 | S | 11100 | | | | |
| G | 00111 | T | 11011 | 00110 | | 01111 | 11101 |
| H | 01000 | U | 11010 | | | | |
| I | 01001 | V | 11001 | | | | |
| J | 01010 | W | 11000 | 11011 | | 01000 | 00101 |
| K | 01011 | X | 10111 | | | | |
| L | 01100 | Y | 10110 | | | | |
| M | 01101 | Z | 10101 | 01110 | | 00101 | 11011! |

## Digital vs. Analog

Computers are digital devices — believe it or not, they can only understand two kinds of signals: "off" (ø) or "on" (1). Computers have to use digital languages, in which each of the 26 letters of the alphabet is represented by a different combination of zeros and ones, called a binary code. A light switch is a good example of what digital signals are like. A light can be on (1) or off (ø), but you can flick the switch on and off in certain patterns to send a "secret code" to your neighbor across the street — just as long as you know the secret code! Sound, on the other hand, is analog. This means that its signals travel on many different levels or in waves. An analog signal works like a light dimmer. Signals can be turned up or turned down, quickly or slowly, in the same way that you can raise or lower your voice.

# The Tune-Up

To get your computer trip into cyberspace off to a smooth start, you need a good tune-up. This means making sure that your computer, keyboard, mouse, modem, and phone line are properly connected so they can talk to each other and work as a team. Here are the right connections:

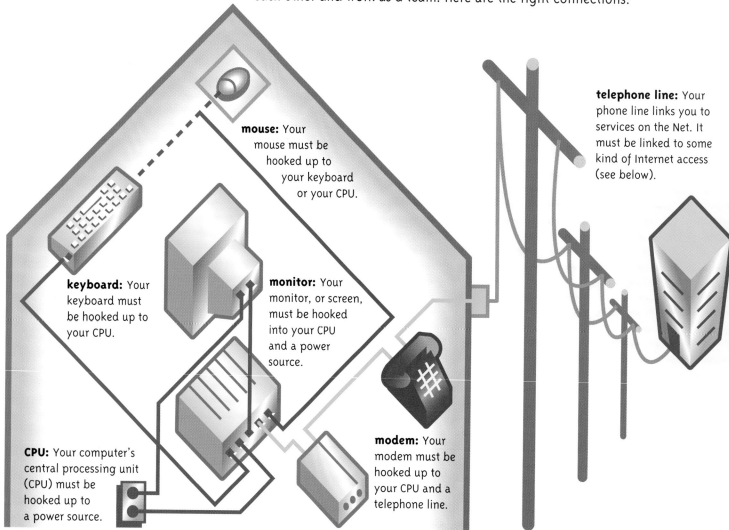

**mouse:** Your mouse must be hooked up to your keyboard or your CPU.

**telephone line:** Your phone line links you to services on the Net. It must be linked to some kind of Internet access (see below).

**keyboard:** Your keyboard must be hooked up to your CPU.

**monitor:** Your monitor, or screen, must be hooked into your CPU and a power source.

**CPU:** Your computer's central processing unit (CPU) must be hooked up to a power source.

**modem:** Your modem must be hooked up to your CPU and a telephone line.

**You have been part of a network for many years and you probably didn't even know it! Every time you pick up the phone, dial a number, and connect to a person on the other end, you enter the network of the telephone system.**

Once you're all hooked up, the next step is making sure your computer "speaks" the special Internet computer language called **TCP/IP** (Transmission Control Protocol/Internet Protocol). All computers on the Net must speak this language so that they can "talk" to each other. How do computers learn this new and important Net language? They learn it from you! You teach your computer everything it needs to know about Net protocol by installing TCP/IP communication software disks on your computer.

Once the program disks are installed on your CPU, you're ready to log on to the Net. One way is to first connect or dial in to a **host** computer that links you to the Internet. Host computers are sometimes owned by companies called **service providers*** that let you access their Net computers for a fee. This way is just like travelling by bus: you pay a bus company to take you where you want to go. Another way people (usually large companies or groups) get on the Net is by direct access. In this case, their own computer is powerful enough to be a **server**, which is its own host linked to the Net. It's like driving a car: you go on your own. The type of access you have doesn't really matter. What's important is that you can get to the Net!

* For a note to parents on finding a service provider, see p. 56.

# Life in the Fast Lane

On the I-Way there aren't any roads — at least not real roads. The travelling takes place over telephone cables. Inside a regular phone cable are twisted pairs of copper wires. These wires carry telephone conversations around the world. At points along the way, signals need to be amplified, or given a boost, so that they can make long-distance journeys.

*Copper wires (far left), covered in colored plastic and twisted together in pairs, carry telephone conversations through regular phone cable.*

*Optical fibers (near left) allow high-speed laser light pulses to carry many more signals farther and faster.*

Cable containing thin glass strands called **optical fibers** is sometimes used instead of cable made up of twisted copper wires. A fiber-optic system uses high-speed laser light pulses to carry voice, data, and picture signals from point to point through the optical fibers. Fiber-optic cables are smaller and lighter than copper phone lines, because an optical fiber is no bigger than a strand of human hair. They send signals faster and farther without the need for amplification. A single strand of optical fiber can support more than 8000 two-way telephone conversations — that's more than 1300 times the data a standard copper phone line can carry. As more and more sections of the Net get hooked up with optical fibers, life in the fast lane will become even faster. V-v-v-r-r-o-o-m!

# Finding the On-Ramps

Some kids have access to the Internet on their own home computers and some kids don't. If you're not hooked up to the Net, there are other ways to get online. Here are some of them:

• A good place to try is your school. Ask your teacher, librarian, or principal about the computers in your classroom or computer lab. Do they have access to the Internet already?

• Some public libraries let members access the Internet from their computers. Check out the library nearest you to see about public Internet access.

• Some science and technology museums have exhibits about the Internet that offer you a chance to check out cyberspace. Call the museum in your area and see if any "cyberdisplays" are going on.

• Computer stores sometimes offer a chance to check out the Net on their computers. Give your local computer store a call. They just may be a one-stop-"surf"-and-shop location.

• You can ask a friend who is hooked up to the Internet at home to let you come over to check it out. Making pals with someone who has a hooked-up computer can lead to making cyberpals on the Net.

## See the Light

Plants are optical devices — if you look at them in a certain light! Plants collect light for energy and to reproduce. Scientists are taking a closer look at how plants use the sun to see if they can shed some light on better use of fiber-optic cables (cables that use light energy) on the Net. Many plants that grow on the dark tropical forest floor have thousands of minuscule lenses covering their surfaces. These lenses, shaped like magnifying glasses, focus light down inside the leaves. From the leaves, light passes to the plant's stem, where long pipe-shaped cells funnel the sunlight to the areas that need it. These long pipes look and act like fiber-optic cables. But in the plants, the system seems to work even better than in fiber optics. Scientists are still not sure why. They're studying optics in plants to get "bright" ideas about fiber optics for the Net.

## Fast Facts on the I-Way

• There are more than 2,000,000 host computers hooked up to the Internet.

• More than 40,000,000 users are already on the I-Way.

• Each month, another 2,000,000 users add on.

• 35,000 new files are added to the Net each day.

• The Internet is made up of over 20,000 different networks.

• A new network connects to the Net every 10 minutes — that's 144 every day, and 1008 in a week!

• By the year 2000, kids will probably spend as much time at the computer as watching TV.

## CYBERJAM

Take a look at these five kids. For some reason, only one of them can get on the Net. Can you see what's jamming up the rest of them? (Answers on page 56.)

# CYBERSTORY

## Winging It on the Net

Each year, thousands of delicate monarch butterflies flutter silently from Canada to Mexico and back. As they migrate up and down the whole length of the continent, hundreds of scientists, teachers, and kids are tracking them on the Internet. These people, who are participating in a special project called Monarch Watch, are winging onto the Net in the name of science. For years scientists have wondered about monarch butterflies and their pattern of migration. There are several monarch mysteries — how far do monarchs fly, which routes do they take, and why do they select those routes? Thanks to Monarch Watch, kids from as far north as Canada and as far south as Mexico have been working to help scientists answer these questions. Kids in classrooms everywhere are keeping their eyes open for monarch sightings, recording the numbers on monarch tags, and sending their findings to other kids and scientists on the Net. Scientists use this information to keep up-to-date on the numbers and paths of monarchs during their migration. Orley "Chip" Taylor, director of Monarch Watch, says the project is "really flying!"

*Chip Taylor (above) and kids all over North America (left) send monarch butterfly reports flying all around the Net.*

**INTERNET ADDRESS**
**http://129.237.246.134/**

19

# Goodbye Snail-mail, Hello E-mail

You've heard about "snail-mail," right? That's the usual way to send a letter — paper, pen, envelope, stamp. Why do cybersurfers call it snail-mail? Because it's s-o-o-o s-l-o-o-o-w! If you send snail-mail to your buddy in France, for example, you must write the letter, stuff it in an envelope, put your address and your buddy's on the front, and slap on a stamp. Then, you walk over to the closest mail box, toss in your letter — THUMP!— and go home to wait. You could wait for days, maybe even weeks, before your pal gets your letter, reads it, and writes back.

Say "Goodbye snail-mail, hello e-mail." The fastest way to send a letter anywhere in the world is through the Net. With electronic mail, or **e-mail** for short, your modem can send messages around the Net in just a few seconds. Type a letter on your computer, zip it across the Net to the computer of the person you're trying to reach, and you can be sure that it gets there before you even have time to yawn.

E-mail is quick and lots of fun. And it's the most popular thing of all to do on the Net. In this chapter, you'll find out how to talk to cyberpals on the Net. There's a new language of symbols you should learn, a **netiquette** to follow, and some hot flames that you should be aware of. So read on, and get the message.

# Who Are You?

In real life, there might be several people in the world with the same name as you — maybe even hundreds. But on the Net, no two users can have the same name. Each user is known by an e-mail address. An e-mail address is a lot like a telephone number — just as there's a different number for every telephone, there's a different e-mail address for every person on the Net.

At first an e-mail address looks like a bowl of alphabet soup. All the letters, numbers, dots, and symbols couldn't possibly make any sense, right? Well, believe it or not, they do. Just as the combination of area code and numbers tells you a lot about where a telephone is located, an e-mail address reveals a lot about who the user is and where the message is coming from. But beware — some people enjoy "spamming," or using your e-mail address to pull a Net prank on someone else! You wouldn't give your phone number to a stranger you meet on the street, and you should also be careful with your e-mail address when dealing with strangers on the Net — but more about that later.

**Reality Byte**

Even though there are millions of computers on the Net, you can usually find who you're looking for. To search for someone's address on the Net, you can use a program called Netfind.
INTERNET ADDRESS
http://www.nova.edu/Inter-Links/netfind.html

# Anatomy of an Address

Any time you see an Internet address — online, in a magazine, here, or in the "Yellow Pages" Directory (starting on page 57) — it will be a string of letters, numbers, symbols, and sometimes words. Type every character into your computer exactly as you see it. Keep the characters all on one line, even if the address runs over two lines on the page. And don't leave any spaces — Internet addresses never contain spaces.

Take a look at the e-mail address below. When you read it aloud, the address is pronounced: "newbie at cyberguide dot surfcity dot e-d-u." Sounds strange, doesn't it? But it's actually a lot like a regular address, with periods or "dots" separating the different elements. So let's take a look at what this address means — just so you know what you're seeing and saying.

## newbie@cyberguide.surfcity.edu

| At the beginning of the address is the user ID, the identity of the person sending or receiving the message. It can be a name written in letters, a series of numbers, or a combination of both. In this case, the person is identified as "newbie." | The "at" symbol is one of the most important symbols in an e-mail address. It separates the user ID to the left of it from the location to the right of it. | This tells you where the user is. It could be the name of a school, office, club, or organization. In this case, newbie is at "cyberguide." | In most cases, this part of the e-mail address is the geographic location, called the **subdomain**. In this example, cyberguide is located in a place called "surfcity." | This is the user's **domain**. It tells you what kind of user this is. In this case, "edu" means that cyberguide is an educational institution. |
|---|---|---|---|---|

# The Domain Name

Every e-mail address is organized with information about the user and the location of the computer in the same place. This way of organizing is called the domain name system, and it makes it easier to look for people on the Net — and to remember their addresses.

If you know a user's name, then you're off to a good start because that's what usually is to the left of the @ symbol in the address. To the right of the @ symbol is where you find out the computer's location, or its domain. As well as where the user is located, the domain tells you what kind of user is there — an individual, a school, a business, or a government. So the last groups of letters on the right-hand side make looking for someone easier by pinpointing what and where the user is. Here are some possible choices:

| | |
|---|---|
| com | commercial (usually businesses) |
| edu | education (schools, universities, etc.) |
| org | other organizations |
| net | networks (like service providers) |
| mil | military (armed forces like the army or navy) |
| gov | governmental organizations |
| on.ca | Ontario, Canada (two-letter abbreviations of province or country names — for example, *us* for the United States, *au* for Australia — are often included in the domain) |

## NAME THE DOMAIN GAME

Billy-Bob lives in Ontario, Canada, and attends J.Brown Public School. From school, he sends an e-mail message to Smiley-Sue. If Smiley-Sue belongs to the Kid Computer Club in Australia, what are the correct e-mail addresses for these two kids? (Answer on page 56.)

**A** To: SmileySue@au.kidclub
From: BillyBob@jbrown.on.edu

**C** To: SmileySue@kidclub.au
From: BillyBob@jbrown.edu

**B** To: SmileySue@kidclub.au.mil
From: BillyBob@jbrown.ca.edu

### Your Address or Mine?

What happens if the Internet runs out of addresses to give to new users? This is exactly what Internet experts are starting to ask themselves. The Internet Network Information Center (InterNIC) gives out Internet Protocol (IP) addresses to networks joining the Net. But because of all the new people who want to get on the Net, there may be a shortage of new addresses one day. So what can InterNIC do? Well, they're trying to change the kinds of addresses people have on the Net so that more combinations of numbers and letters are available. They haven't solved the problem yet, but they're working on it.

The **To** line is the address of the person receiving the message. If the address on this line is incorrect, the message will be returned.

The **From** line contains the address of the person sending the message.

The **Subject** line tells you what the message is about in a few words.

**Attachments** are files that you add to your e-mail message. An attachment can be anything — a story, a picture, a game — you want to pass along on the Net.

The **Message** is the "letter" part of the e-mail. It can be as long as you like. But be nice on the Net, or you might get flamed!

# Anatomy of E-mail

You can send e-mail from your computer to anyone who has an e-mail address any place in the world. E-mail is faster than regular mail — it only takes a few seconds! — and electronic letters rarely get lost.

Once you've seen one piece of e-mail you've seen them all! All e-mail looks exactly the same, because it follows a standard format, or protocol, that all computers on the Net can understand. Here's how it all works:

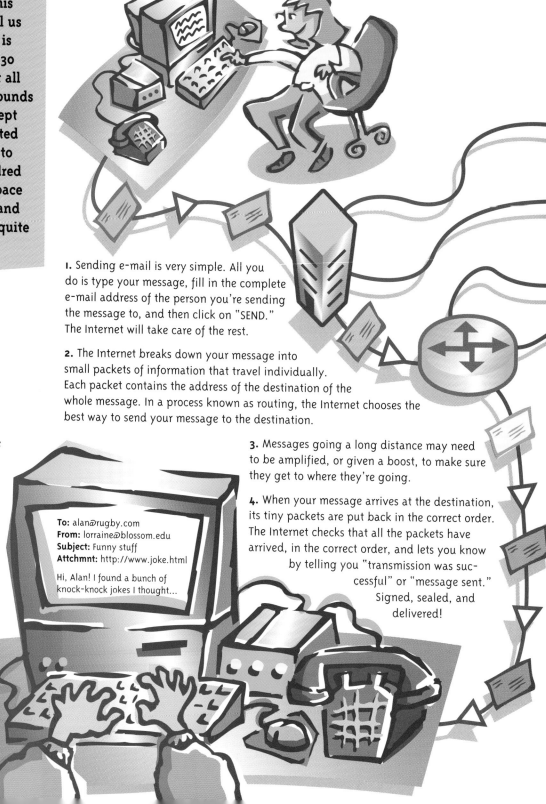

To: alan@rugby.com
From: lorraine@blossom.edu
Subject: Funny stuff
Attchmnt: http://www.joke.html

Hi, Alan! I found a bunch of knock-knock jokes I thought...

**1.** Sending e-mail is very simple. All you do is type your message, fill in the complete e-mail address of the person you're sending the message to, and then click on "SEND." The Internet will take care of the rest.

**2.** The Internet breaks down your message into small packets of information that travel individually. Each packet contains the address of the destination of the whole message. In a process known as routing, the Internet chooses the best way to send your message to the destination.

**3.** Messages going a long distance may need to be amplified, or given a boost, to make sure they get to where they're going.

**4.** When your message arrives at the destination, its tiny packets are put back in the correct order. The Internet checks that all the packets have arrived, in the correct order, and lets you know by telling you "transmission was successful" or "message sent." Signed, sealed, and delivered!

# Netiquette and Flames

When you speak to someone face to face or on the phone, it's usually easy to tell when they're joking and when they're not. But on the Net, where you communicate by messages on a computer screen, it's not so easy. And you might send e-mail to people you've never met — so they may not understand the way you express yourself or your sense of humor. Getting along with others on the Net requires rules of netiquette. If you don't follow them you might get **flamed** — receive a barrage of negative responses to your rude behavior —and then it could get difficult to cool things down!

• Using **boldface** or <u>underlined</u> type is not a good idea. While these may look good on your screen, chances are the computer you're sending your message to will be unable to read them.

• On the Net, TYPING A SENTENCE IN CAPITAL LETTERS, LIKE THIS, IS LIKE SHOUTING, and it's considered very rude. Type in caps only if you are very angry, or only a word or two if you're expressing a very STRONG point.

• When you receive an e-mail message, try to answer it as soon as possible. Since the message only took a few seconds to get to you, why should it take weeks before you reply?

• E-mail makes it easy — too easy — to send a message you might regret later. Swearing, name-calling, and general rudeness are absolute no-no's on the Net. If you forget your manners, you'll get flamed back — you'll be bombarded with angry messages from unhappy people on the Net. Sorting through a mailbox full of complaints is no fun. So remember: "Sticks and stones may break your bones, but flames could really hurt you!"

# Say It with a "Smiley" :-)

If you're being funny on the Net, or just want to have some fun, try an **emoticon**. Emoticons show your feelings on faces made up of symbols and letters from your keyboard. Here are a few to help *say* it with a smiley — just tilt your head to the left to *see* it with a smiley!

| | |
|---|---|
| :-) | Smiley |
| :-o | Wow! |
| :-c | Totally unbelievable! |
| :-I | Hmmm… |
| '-) | Wink |
| :^D | Great idea! |
| :-* | Ooops! |
| :-( | Frown |
| :-, | Smirk |
| :-V | Shout |
| :-r | Tongue hangin' out |
| :-& | Tongue tied |
| :-T | Keeping a straight face |
| :-D | Big smile |
| :-# | My lips are sealed! |
| I-{ | Good grief! |

| | |
|---|---|
| :-} | Yum-Yum! |
| 8-o | No way! |
| (-: | I'm left-handed! |
| %-) | Bug-eyed |
| 8-) | I wear glasses |
| :-[) | Moustache |

| | |
|---|---|
| ;-) | Crying |
| :-@ | Screaming |
| I-I | Sleeping |
| I-0 | Yawning |
| :-S | I'm totally confused! |
| :-/ | Skeptical |
| 3:) | My pet |
| C:# | Football player |
| :-() | Ouch! |
| {:-) | Wearing stereo headphones |
| <:-D | It's my birthday! |
| ~~:-( | Just got flamed! |
| :) | Ha-ha! |
| I-) | Hee-hee! |
| I-D | Ho-ho! |
| :-> | Hey-hey! |

# Acronyms FYI — For Your Information

On the Net you may see abbreviations of common expressions or sayings. People use these just for fun, or to save time. Here's a list of some popular Net acronyms. So the next time someone says BFN, you know to say CYA!

| | |
|---|---|
| BBL | Be back later |
| BFN | Bye for now |
| BRB | Be right back |
| BTW | By the way |
| CYA | See ya! |

| | |
|---|---|
| FWIW | For what it's worth |
| FYI | For your information |
| IAE | In any event |
| IMHO | In my humble opinion |
| IMO | In my opinion |
| IOW | In other words |
| ITC | It's the coolest! |
| JFYI | Just for your information |
| LMHO | Laughing my head off |
| LOL | Laughing out loud |
| NBD | No big deal |
| NOYB | None of your business |
| OIC | Oh, I see… |
| OTL | Out to lunch |
| OTOH | On the other hand |
| PMFJI | Pardon me for jumping in |

| | |
|---|---|
| ROFL | Rolling on the floor laughing |
| RS | Real soon |
| TIA | Thanks in advance |
| TIC | Tongue in cheek |
| TTFN | Ta-ta for now |
| TTYL | Talk to you later |
| TWF | That was fun |
| YMBJ | You must be joking! |
| WYSIWYG | What you see is what you get |

## Writing on the Walls

Emoticons are fun symbols to use on the Net. But reading pictures is not a new idea. Ancient Egyptians wrote with hieroglyphics, or picture symbols, as long ago as 3000 B.C. Hieroglyphics were carved and painted onto the stone walls of Egyptian towns and tombs. But hieroglyphics are harder to read than emoticons — each picture represents a sound, not the whole idea or emotion that a smiley communicates. In fact, the secret of deciphering hieroglyphics was a mystery for centuries after ancient Egyptian civilization ended. Finally, in 1799, a tablet called the Rosetta Stone was unearthed. It was inscribed with one message in three languages — Greek, later Egyptian, and hieroglyphics. After years of decoding, Egyptologists learned to read the pictures as easily as you read your A-B-Cs!

## INTERACT

### "I HEAR YA!"

Joshua sent e-mail messages to Max, Wendy, Eva, and Basil to find out if they wanted to get together to see *Adrenal Pump*, a new action movie. Take a look at the replies below and see if you can figure out who went to the movie with Joshua and who did not. (Answer on page 56.)

YMBJ! I heard the movie was NBD.
Max

If Basil's going, I'm not. He always talks during the movie and it drives me CRAZY! :-( Otherwise I'd love to. BFN
Wendy

I heard ITC! BTW, I just spoke to Wendy and, FYI, I don't talk during movies! TTYL.
Basil

Sounds good to me, but I'm not sure if can make it. IOW it depends on Max. If he's going, I'll catch a ride to the theatre with his dad. If he's not then I won't either. BTW, when does the movie start? CYA.
Eva 8-)

Hundreds of emoticons exist, and people are making up new ones all the time. In fact, there are whole books of smileys out there. How many can you come up with on your own? Now your e-mail can really be face to face!

# CYBERSTORIES

## CYBERPALS AROUND THE WORLD

Some kids send and receive e-mail just for fun. Others use e-mail to save orangutans, to plan and build a new city, or to make cyberpals from a hospital bed, too.

## Going Ape

The kids at Pasir Ridge International School in Kalimantan, Indonesia, are using cyberspace to help save orangutans. These kids started an adopt-an-orangutan program to help the Orangutan Reintroduction Project in their area. The Pasir Ridge kids got students from other classrooms around the world to "adopt" orangutans by donating money to the project. In exchange, the kids at Pasir Ridge work closely with the people at the orangutan center to make sure that the money is spent on giving the orangutans the care they need. Then they e-mail progress reports, via the Internet, to kids around the world.

At Pasir Ridge School, students use e-mail to keep kids around the world posted on the baby orangutans they "adopt."

The Orangutan Reintroduction Project takes care of young orangutans until they can be released into the wild.

## City in Cyberspace

How did kids from cities at either end of North America work together to build a new city? Through e-mail! The CitySpace project involved students aged 9–16 from the Exploratorium in San Francisco and from the Ontario Science Centre in Toronto. These kids used e-mail to communicate as they planned the "construction" of a city on the Net. They formed roadwork crews, teams of engineers, and waterworks departments to decide everything about their new city — its exact size; all the road, bus, train, and subway systems needed to keep the citizens moving; the houses, schools, hospitals, and airports; the utilities; and all the other components of a working city. The buildings and other city pieces were constructed in 3D on computers at school, home, or the project site, and then were added to the CitySpace model on a powerful computer. When their city was complete, the kids "flew" around it in cybercrafts called "HoverBoys," meeting up with their cyberpals from across the continent.

INTERNET ADDRESS
http://cityspace.org/

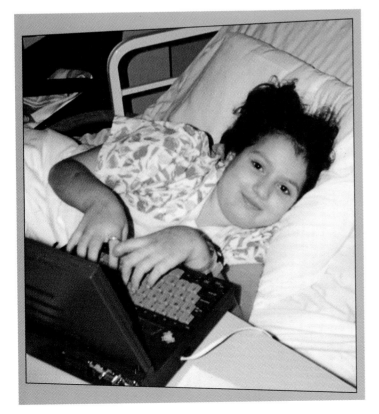

## Kids Hop from Hospital to the Net

Just because you are sick or disabled doesn't mean you can't hop around on the Net. Dr. Arlette Lefebvre, nicknamed "Dr. Froggy," realized that kids in the hospital can feel pretty cut off from the rest of the world. So she set up a network to link sick and disabled kids with people and information around the world through e-mail. Making cyberpals with other kids and adults is fun, and it helps sick kids feel better. They can meet in cyberspace to share ideas and experiences, even if it's impossible for them to get together in person. More than 5000 kids are playing and learning on the Ability OnLine network, and e-mailing into cyberspace is exactly what the doctor ordered!

INTERNET ADDRESS
info@ablelink.org

# Surfing the Net

Sending and receiving e-mail is one fun thing you can do on the Net, but **surfing** the Net is where it's really at. Surfing the Net means hopping onto the Internet's digital waves and riding the computer network to just about any place in the world. Surfers cruise between computers, databases, and forums around the globe, moving from site to site, in search of the perfect wave . . . er . . . file.

You can log on at the computer in your home, hook up to the Louvre Museum in Paris, jump over to the United Nations in New York, then check out the latest version of your favorite video game — all in the time it takes to suck a cough drop! Getting, sending, and receiving information from the Net can take only a few seconds, as long as you know how to surf.

Surfing the Net, or being able to find what you're looking for, takes a bit of practice. There's so much information on the Net, and so many places to go to get it, that you may not know where to start. Then there's the problem of knowing how to get to where you want to go, once you've decided what you're looking for! But have no fear, this chapter tells you all you need to know about surfing the Net — without ever getting wet. Surf's up, dude!

# Just Go for It!

Whenever you do anything for the first time — say, diving into a swimming pool — you feel scared, then excited, and then thrilled that you actually did it. Hopping onto the Internet is no different. It can be a bit scary at first, and maybe even a bit overwhelming. But once you're on the Net — chatting with people you've never met, browsing through a library in a foreign country, or tapping into the latest results of a space mission — you'll be glad you did. The key to learning how to surf the Net is this: just go for it.

## Radical "Surf"ware

Once you have a computer hooked up to the Net, the first thing you need to really get surfing is a special software program, called a Net **browser**. This computer program is designed to make surfing the Net a lot easier for you. Today most browsers let you use your mouse to point-and-click at the places you want to explore and then — like magic — your computer takes you there. Of course, it wasn't always so easy. Even a few years ago, you had to know complicated UNIX commands, and you had to type in every character of an address, just to get where you wanted to go. Not any more. Anyone who has a good browser, or "surf"ware, loaded into their computer can hop on and catch the digital waves. Totally radical, dude!

To get a Net browser you usually have to go to a computer store and buy one. But many service providers will set you up with one. And luckily, there are all sorts of programs, including browsers, on the Net that you can transfer to your computer or try out for free — freeware and shareware programs. Click on the Hot Stuff box on your Cyber Blastoff disk to find out more about software you can grab from the Net.

## A Web of Waves

Once you start exploring the Net in search of cool things to see, download, and explore, it won't be long before you get caught in the **WWW**, or the World Wide Web. It's called the Web, for short, and it's the main reason surfing the Net has become so popular for millions of scientists, teachers, business people, adults, and kids around the world. It's a part of the Net that's great because it's easy to use. The Web uses graphics and hypertext, and these make all the difference when it comes to smooth surfing.

## Grab Graphics and Hyper Surf

Web graphics are more than just pretty pictures that can move around or spin on your computer screen! The pictures, called icons, allow you to click with your mouse instead of typing in commands. Icons are a serious bonus when it comes to surfing the Net because you just point-and-click at certain commands without having to spell them out for your computer. If you can see the icons on your screen and can click your mouse, then you've got what it takes to surf the Web of waves.

**Hypertext** makes surfing the Net hyper-easy. With hypertext, certain words are underlined or appear in color on your computer screen. These words are linked automatically to related information somewhere else on the Web. To get to this information, you click on the hypertext words with your mouse and your computer jumps to a new site. Let's say you're on the Web reading about monk seals at a zoo Web site. You read: "Monk seals are protected in the Frigate Shoals off the coast of the Hawaiian Islands . . . ." If the words Frigate Shoals are hypertext, clicking on those words with your mouse will get you more information about where they are — and this information might be posted by a tourist office in Hawaii!

### Web Text

**Browser:** special software that lets you surf or "browse" through the Net, and especially the Web, by letting you use your mouse to point-and-click at icons instead of typing in commands

**Home Page:** a page or screen that a site on the Web uses as its main base or home

**Hypertext:** text that appears underlined or in a different color on your screen. Clicking on hypertext will automatically link you to other documents, sites, and information on the Web that's related to that subject

**Hypertext Markup Language, or HTML:** a computer language used by programmers to design Web Home Pages

**Hypertext Transfer Protocol, or HTTP:** a special computer code used by programmers that makes it possible for users to get and see documents on the Web

**Site:** a place you visit on the Web, usually starting with the Home Page, that's filled with lots of things to check out

**Uniform Resource Locator, or URL:** the address for a site on the Web

HAWAII TOURISM

# Catchin' the URL waves!

The first thing you need to know about surfing the Web is how to catch the waves — the digital waves, that is! To get to specific Web sites, you'll need to know their addresses. On the Web, an address is called an **URL**, a uniform resource locator. Like the e-mail addresses we saw in the previous chapter, an URL might be hard to understand at first. But once you know what all the letters, symbols, and slashes stand for, the address will url . . . err . . . roll off your tongue.

## http://www.cybersurfer.edu/surfing.html

| This tells you that the site is on the World Wide Web. Over the next few years, URLs might drop this prefix. | // Anything after these two slashes indicates the computer on the Web where the site is located. | / Anything after the single slash identifies a specific file, or a directory of information at the site. | This means that the file is especially formatted for the Web. |

## TALK THE TALK

Net wizards *boot the box, surf the Net,* and then *gronk out.* What does that mean? On a piece of paper, match up the meanings below on the left with the Net words on the right, and try to *crack the ice!* You'll find most of the terms somewhere in this chapter, and the answers are on page 56.

| | | | |
|---|---|---|---|
| 1 | place where computers "talk" on the Net | A | ice |
| 2 | computers linked to others to form a network | B | barf mail |
| 3 | computer | C | net |
| 4 | start up | D | newbie |
| 5 | computer code | E | online |
| 6 | break a computer code | F | gronk out |
| 7 | electronic mail | G | newsie |
| 8 | regular mail | H | eyeball search |
| 9 | electronic junk mail | I | box |
| 10 | the state of being on the Net | J | e-mail |
| 11 | a new user on the Net | K | cyberspace |
| 12 | a newsgroup junkie | L | crack |
| 13 | read a computer screen | M | snail mail |
| 14 | travel from site to site in cyberspace | N | surf |
| 15 | to say, "That's enough, I'm going home!" | O | boot |

# Home Sweet Home . . .

When you get to a site on the Web, the first thing you'll see is a Home Page. This is where you start exploring a site. Some Home Pages have lots of photos or graphics and others don't. Some have a lot of hypertext areas and others don't. But the one thing that every Home Page has in common is that it says, "Welcome to our cyberhome!" Here's an example of what a Home Page might look like.

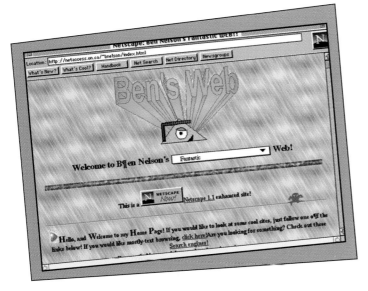

*Ben Nelson, 13, lives on the World Wide Web. Well, he doesn't really live there, but he does have his own "home" in cyberspace — a Home Page, that is!*

A Home Page can be as long as you want it to be. Ben's takes up more than three screens as you scroll down. On the first screen, Ben welcomes you and lets you choose a description of what you see: Fantastic, Incredible, Beautiful, or Fantastically Well Made. (Humble, isn't he?) The second screen lets you visit different sections of the site to do some cool stuff: send e-mail, play games, learn more about Ben, chat in real time. It also tells you how many people have visited Ben's Home Page before you — Ben makes a joke that the counter is wrong, and that a lot more people than *that* have checked out his site.

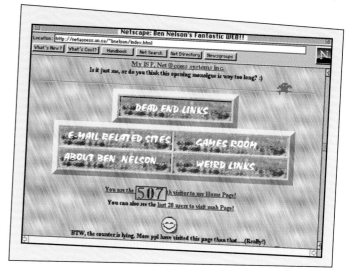

On the third screen, Ben suggests some of the more popular things to do when you visit him at his cyber-home. For example, you can play Hairball, a game Ben invented, and chase a crazy cat through a large hotel in Ben's home town. Ben ends up by inviting you to e-mail your comments to him, if only to let him know how many spelling mistakes or stray ¶s you can find. Ben Nelson's Fantastic Home Page is loads of interactive fun, and has made him lots of cyberpals. But be warned: it will probably look totally different by the time you go there, since he's redesigning it all the time!

# Ben's Cyberhome

After checking out Ben Nelson's Home Page, we had a few questions for him. Here's what the cyberkid had to say about the Net.

### What's your Home Page all about?
There is no real purpose to my Home Page. It's just there for fun and it's telling everybody "Hey look, I made a Home Page!"

### What made you start your own Home Page?
I wanted to do something that was different and I wanted to be interactive. People e-mail me saying how cool my Home Page is or how many spelling mistakes it has . . .

### What's on your Home Page?
I have lots of games on my page — games that I made up myself!

### Where did you learn how to make games and a Home Page?
My dad helped me a bit. He started me off with HTML [see *Web Text* on page 33]. At first HTML looked kind of complicated, but it's actually pretty easy. Once I got the hang of it, I was able to program my page.

### How long have you been "surfing" the Net?
A little over a year.

### What do you like about the Net?
Basically you can go anywhere you want and see all sorts of cool stuff. If you have a browser, then you can just click and go to all sorts of Home Pages.

### What stuff do you look for?
Just fun stuff. Stuff on TV shows, games . . . anything fun. I just go to different places when I surf the Net. I don't really know where I'm going or what I expect to find, but I just go around the Net checking out different things.

## Reality Byte

There's a lot of really useful stuff for you to get from the Net, but there are also lots of oddball things to see and do. You can watch the tide roll in on a beach in California, see how many cups a virtual coffee machine is brewing, or order a virtual pizza right to your computer screen. Why would you bother to do any of these things? Because you can! Check out the CyberStops in the "Yellow Pages" Directory (pages 57–72) or on your Cyber Blastoff disk for more BYC sites!

### How do you "check things out" on the Web?

The one thing you need to know is the URL. An URL is like an address, like a street address, that tells you where a site is located. It's impossible to know the URL for every cool site on the Web because there are millions! I find what I'm looking for with a **search engine**.

### What's a search engine?

A search engine lets you search for sites by typing words into the computer. Let's say you wanted to look up "cool stuff." You type in those two words — "cool" and "stuff" — and the search engine will look it up for you.

### How many sites have you been to?

Thousands. I keep a "bookmark file" of all the places on the Net that I really like and want to go to again. I keep adding more sites, or bookmarks, to my file. There's so much cool stuff on the Net that it's hard to remember them all in your brain. You can add a bookmark, which is really just the address of a site, into the file on your computer, and then when you click on the bookmark in the file, you'll get there.

### What's the best thing on the Net?

The TV Home Pages, other people's Home Pages, and the fact that I can just click on anything and go anywhere. There are some bad pages on the Net, pages that aren't so suitable for kids. My dad says to me: "Ben, stay clear of those." So I do.

### Any advice for newbies?

First of all, the Net will not come out and bite you. There's no reason to be afraid of the Internet. Just go out and visit some Home Pages!

### How much time do you spend surfing the Net?

About 60 hours a month. I mostly surf after school. Sometimes in the evenings, if I have no homework or if nothing good is on TV . . .

### Do you think you'd like a "cyber-career" when you're older?

Yes. Or maybe I'll become a teacher.

INTERNET ADDRESS
http:/netaccess.on.ca/~bnelson/index.html

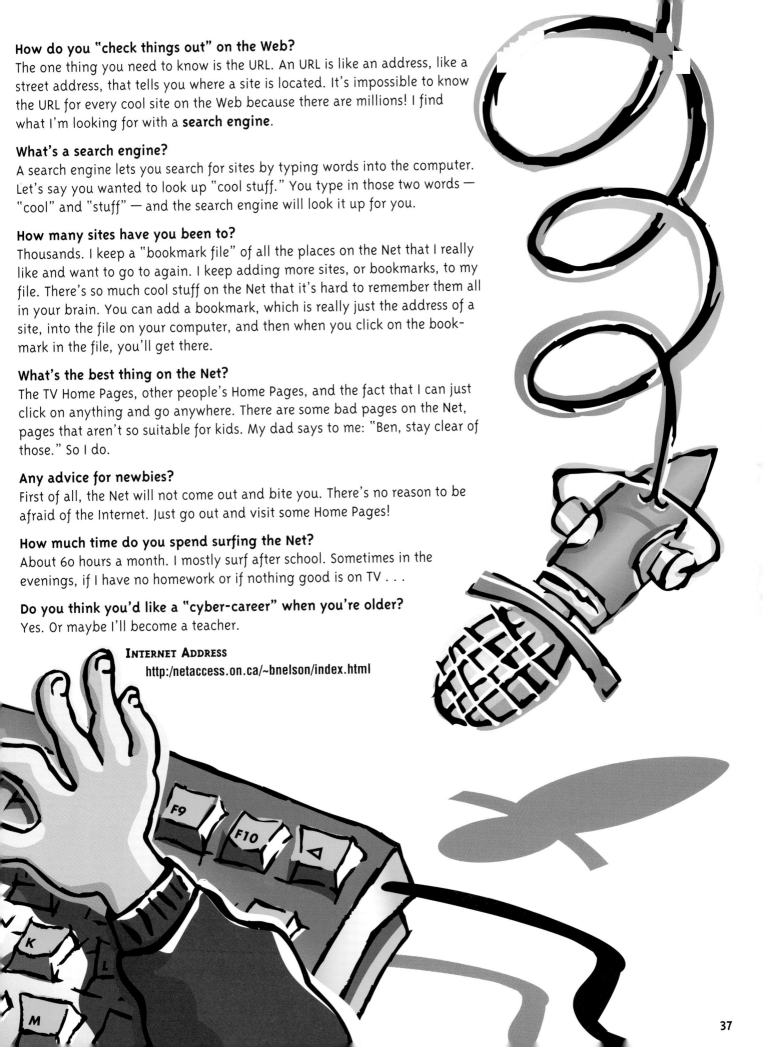

# A Surfer's Paradise

The Net is full of hot topics, cool sites, and plenty of "I-can't-believe-I'm-here!" places to explore. You can ride the digital Internet waves to just about anywhere in the world. You can tell the Amphibian Task Force in Peru how many frogs you saw in your pond, tell TV producers what you thought of their latest show, find out the birthday of an animal you just saw at the zoo, or tell NASA what you think about the possibilities of Earthlings living in space. The Net is a paradise of information because everything is accessible to everyone. Every file, picture, or bit of information on the Net is available for you to read, look at, or keep. Take a look at how you can surf through info paradise and catch the perfect file.

# The Lowdown on Downloading

There will be lots of stuff on the Net that you will want to keep on hand in your own computer, and that's where FTP, or File Transfer Protocol, comes in. An FTP program lets you transfer, or **download**, information in many forms from another computer to your own. **FTP sites** are computers where Internet files — articles, photos, video games, movie clips — are stored electronically, just as books, magazines, and videotapes are stored physically on the shelves in a library. There are more than 1200 FTP sites on the Net that hold millions of free files that are yours for the taking. But how do you find the right file?

# Surfing With Archie

An **Archie** server is a program on the Net that acts like a librarian. It keeps track of the files in FTP sites. Some Archies keep track of all the FTP sites in the world, others index the FTP sites in one area. An Archie makes finding files to download easy: all you have to do is type in a word, and the Archie will tell you the addresses of all the files on that topic. There are more than 30 Archie servers in the world, and together they cover the entire Internet.

# Surfing Gopherspace

FTP sites aren't the only places to find neat stuff on the Net. If you want to "go-fer" information on any kind of computer on the Net, then blast off into Gopherspace! That's where **Gopher** programs do their work, helping you look through computers to find information anywhere on the Net. Gophers are search tools programmed with built-in Internet roadmaps — they "dig" through the masses of information on the Net, finding the quickest way for you to get to the files you want.

There are more than 1600 Gophers to choose from, and each of these Gophers specializes in a certain subject area or in a different part of the world. No matter what topic you are interested in, a Gopher program will tunnel through the Net and bring back a **menu**, or a list of options. Just like on a restaurant menu, you might find a lot of choices or just a few. Every file in every directory in the world won't be listed — you wouldn't expect to find hamburgers on the menu of every restaurant in town. From the menu, you choose which further menu or computer sites are most likely to have exactly what you're looking for. And then you just "gopher" it!

## Veronica Searches Gophers

When you choose a Gopher to help you search a certain topic, you're using only one of the 1600 Gophers available to help you out. If you really wanted to do a thorough Net search you'd have to search each of the 1600 Gophers one by one — a job that could take more than a week. A program has been designed to search the searching Gophers. It's called Veronica, which stands for **Very Easy Rodent-Oriented Netwide Index to Computerized Archives.** Veronica keeps track of all the Gopher directories and all the Gophers on the Net, and updates the list twice a week. It's a tough job, but somebody's got to do it!

## Real-Time Chats

You can have a live conversation — just like a telephone chat — with someone on the Internet. The only difference is that you're typing instead of speaking. These kinds of conversations are called real-time chats or IRCs, Internet Relay Chats. At first it's a bit difficult to stay on top of IRCs because you and the other person might be typing at the same time. Chatting it up on the Net can be fun, but be careful. Some people may ask you questions during an IRC — like where you live or go to school, where your parents work or what they do — that you really shouldn't answer. If someone is pressing you for personal information, don't panic. Just politely end the conversation — CYA!

# Be a Newsie

What day of the week will your birthday be in the year 2008? How old was Beethoven when he first played the piano? When is the next solar eclipse in Hong Kong? The answer to these and many other questions are available on the Net. You just have to know where to ask them. To find answers or to talk about interesting topics, people turn to **newsgroups**.

Newsgroups form the part of the Net called Usenet. Usenet started in 1979 when Tom Truscott and Jim Ellis, two students at Duke University, hooked up a couple of computers so they could chat online. Since then, newsgroups have formed around more than 10,000 subjects of discussion, and millions of people use them. People just love to talk! And people who get really hooked on newsgroup discussions are called *newsies*.

You can find a newsgroup discussion forum that relates to just about any subject under, over, and around the sun. You can search through a newsgroup library to read messages or discussions that happened yesterday, or you can chat in real time with people around the world. Many newsgroups have FAQ sections, for "frequently asked questions," so you can get up to speed on the subject before jumping in. (Netiquette experts suggest that you always "FAQ check" — that way, you'll be a fully prepared Net newsie.) And the best part is that, no matter who you are, where you live, or how old you are, you can join in everything that's going on.

# Categorically Speaking

Newsgroup categories are typed out in lower-case letters followed by a period. The first part of the newsgroup name tells you what the general category is, and the rest gives you more detail about the group's specific discussion. Here are some of the categories found on the Net:

**comp.** In this category — computers — there are too many newsgroups to even count. This makes sense, considering the discussions are taking place in a network of computer networks.

**soc.** This group deals with social issues, like general culture, dancing, and even life on the I-way.

**news.** This category is about newsgroups themselves, and is a good place for first-timers to begin. Check out *news.newusers.questions* to get started.

**sci.** Here you'll find science groups, including *sci.space*, *sci.medicine*, and others. Subgroups get more specific, like *sci.animals.ferrets*.

**biz.** Business-oriented newsgroups, often relating to a specific company or product, are found here.

**talk.** In this category you can discuss just about any topic in the world. For example, *talk.movies.action* may be all about the latest action flick.

**alt.** Alternative newsgroups cover everything from the strange and bizarre to the silly and boring. Some are worth checking out, some aren't. (You should talk to your parents or a teacher about what's OK for kids here.) Anything goes in this category — there's even one called *alt.aliens.visitors*!

# Unravelling Threads of Conversation

Newsgroups are like electronic meeting rooms where people can meet online and have conversations about different topics. The thing that makes online discussions different from "real" discussions is that everything that people type into the newsgroup stays in the newsgroup's library for a few days. This means that you could go into the newsgroup library and read a discussion, word-for-word as it took place, even though you weren't there.

To find out what people said in a newsgroup, you read through a thread of conversation. Say someone posts this message on a newsgroup: "How can I build a kite?" Someone may reply with her favorite kite design, then another person adds a hint for a more efficient tail, then a third replies with a completely different design, and on and on the thread goes until no one has anything else to say about kites!

## What are you looking for?

The newsgroups on Usenet are divided into categories and sub-categories that cover more than 10,000 different topics all over the Net. So how on Earth can you find anything? Luckily it's not as difficult as it may seem. A newsgroup's name tells you a lot about the subject it covers and that makes it easier to find exactly what you're looking for. For example, a newsgroup about science and space, or about the shuttle in particular, would probably be called something like this: sci.space.shuttle. Makes sense, right? Once you know the codes for the different newsgroup categories, finding one is easier than finding a rollerblade rink in the phone book.

## Reality Byte

Some people just listen to what's being said in a newsgroup but never jump into the discussion. These types of bystanders are called "lurkers."

# CYBERSTORIES

## NET SURFERS

Kids are beginning to surf the Net to explore all sorts of amazing stuff around the world. Some kids even use the Net to take a look at some "out-of-this-world" locations, like deep space. Here are some examples of kid surfers and what they're doing on the Net.

## Pedal Up on the Net

Since February, 1995, bicycling explorers have been making long and difficult journeys through Mexico and Central America to study ancient Mayan ruins. As part of a project called MayaQuest, team members ride their bikes from country to country, exploring one ancient ruin after another. And more than a million kids, teachers, and scientists from all over the world pedal along with them — through the Internet. The MayaQuest Project has set up a Home Page on the World Wide Web so that anyone interested in their findings can log on and check things out. The explorers carry laptop computers and satellite dishes with them as they ride. They use Internet technology to e-mail their daily diaries, answer questions, and send research notes from remote sites to archeologists and students everywhere. Classrooms studying Mayan culture as part of their history, science, math, Spanish, or geography curricula, tap into MayaQuest and become part of the journey. It's like travelling with Indiana Jones online!

The carvings on this ancient Mayan door would take a year to get into print. MayaQuest puts them online in minutes.

INTERNET ADDRESS
http://www.mecc.com/mayaquest.html/

Students (left) check out a map of Mexico and Central America to chart the path of MayaQuest's cycling archeologists (below).

## Space Out with NASA

Want to ask an astronaut some spaced-out questions? Looking for a great shot of planet Earth from the Space Shuttle? More than a thousand people — most of them kids — tap into NASA Spacelink each week to get down-to-earth facts about outer space. Kids get detailed information about space missions, launch schedules, or the latest in space news. Photos taken from the Space Shuttle can be downloaded, and questions for astronauts can be posted in an e-mailbox. Through Spacelink, kids launch into space without ever leaving Earth!

**INTERNET ADDRESS**
http://spacelink.msfc.nasa.gov/

## A Class Act

At an Ottawa, Ontario, high school, teenagers took the Net into their own hands to send a classroom into cyberspace. These students helped create a computer program that includes graphics, e-mail, icons, newsgroups, chat lines, and libraries linked to sites on the Net. The software, called The Virtual Classroom, teaches people how to use the Net in a way that's easy and fun. The Virtual Classroom includes sections like Homework Help, Student/Teacher files, and Fun Stuff. When you click on the icons, the program links you to sites on the Net where you can find the information you need. The Virtual Classroom makes jumping online so much fun that it gets kids surfing around the Net before they know it.

**INTERNET ADDRESS**
info@dwc.com

# The Safety Net

Don't talk to strangers. Look both ways before you cross the street. Don't play with fire. Be careful. Do these safety rules sound familiar? They should, because you've probably heard them over and over again. All kids get the same warnings from parents, teachers, and other people who care. They're giving you one simple message: play it smart no matter what you do.

Wherever you are, being smart helps you to keep safe, and the Internet is no exception. The Internet isn't really a dangerous place. For the most part, it's lots of fun. On the Net, anything goes — that's why you'll find lots of wonderful stuff to see and do. But this freedom also has its flip side.

Just like dangers in the real world, problems on the Net include theft, intruders, nasty messages, hate literature, and people you want to avoid, who may be dishonest or dangerous or both. Because millions of computers on the Net are hooked up to each other, nasty messages from nasty people spread quickly across the Net. Computer illnesses, or **viruses**, are also very contagious. Your computer can "catch" a virus from Japan, for example, and pass it on to a computer in Boston. In just a few seconds, thousands of computers around the world can become "sick."

Luckily, it's easy to have fun and be safe. From buying a virus checker, a program that spots bad bugs, to being careful about the information you share, there are ways for you and your computer to be safe on the Net. This chapter tells you about most of them, but no one can give you all the warnings. The most important thing to remember is this: play it smart no matter what you do.

A long password is harder to remember — but it's also much harder to crack! The greater the number of characters a password contains, the greater the number of combinations a hacker has to try. This hacker math shows that the longer a password is, the more crack-proof it is.

| Number of characters: | Number of combinations: |
| --- | --- |
| 1 | 36 |
| 2 | 1300 |
| 3 | 117,000 |
| 4 | 1,700,000 |
| 5 | 2,000,000,000 |
| 6 | 78,000,000,000 |

## Crack-proof Passwords

1. Never give your password to anyone else. That's like an open invitation to hackers.

2. Don't use obvious passwords, like your name. Hackers will always try those first.

3. Try to choose a password with six characters or more. Check out the Reality Byte above to see why.

4. Select a password that's easy to remember for you, but not for anyone else. Use a combination of letters and numbers that don't make any sense — except to you.

5. Keep your password written down in a secret place. But not so secret that you forget it yourself!

6. Try changing your password from time to time, but always keep crack-proof rules 1–5 in mind when you do.

# Password Please

You can't "lock" your computer the way you lock your front door, but keeping intruders out of your computer is just as important as keeping burglars out of your home. You may not have important files or secret documents to protect, but that doesn't mean a **hacker**, a computer criminal, won't want to break into your computer. You see, if someone uses your ID to get onto the Net, then that person becomes you on the Net. And anything that person does on the Net — good or bad — looks like it's being done by you.

The best security device you have on the Net is your **password**. The key to safety is keeping your password a secret. Most passwords are combinations of 36 common characters: the 26 letters of the English alphabet (A–Z) and the 10 numerals (0–9). Whatever your password is, you want it to be something that a hacker won't **crack**.

Your password might be a combination that you choose to use, it may have come with your software, or it could be a computer-generated combination that was sent to you by mail along with your Internet address. Most people don't need to know their password by heart because it's automatically programmed into their computer to speed up the process of logging on. You can use this kind of password, but make sure you have it written down some place safe because, if you forget it, you could be "locked out" of the Net.

# Be a Street-smart Surfer

### Be cool, not cruel
Play it cool — not cruel — and you'll make more friends than enemies on the Net. Don't be mean to cyberpals and stay away from those who say mean things to you.

### Don't get harmed by a hoax
You can't see who you're talking to on the Net, so adults sometimes pretend to be kids when they're really not. Their hoax can cause you harm — so watch out. Beware of impostors.

### Pick your friends carefully
Kids you meet on the Net might want to meet you in real life. This can be a cool idea — or not. Only arrange to meet kids you've been in e-mail contact with for a while, and pick a public place to meet in, like a park. And always make sure an adult goes to the meeting with you.

### Mum is always the word
It's cool to talk to strangers on the Net, but it's not cool to tell them certain things: your home address or phone number; where you go to school; where your parents work or what they do; or anything else about your family or friends. After all, they're still strangers and they could really hurt you.

### Go for the good, steer clear of the bad
Most kids go on the Net for the same reason you do — to have fun, make friends, and find cool stuff. But there are bad guys on the Net, too. These people fill the Net with nasty messages, horrible pictures, and dangerous information. You'll know what the bad stuff is when you see it, so you should know that it's better to stay away. Stay out of trouble, go for the good, and you'll be a street-smart surfer.

## Don't Flame Me!
One day Gerry Elman, a lawyer in Pennsylvania, logged onto his computer and discovered that he had been a victim of a hacker's curse. His e-mail box was loaded with messages from people all over the world — including Kuwait, South Africa, and Tasmania — telling him that he was no longer welcome on the Net. He had been flamed. Turns out someone had cracked Gerry's password and forged his Internet identity to post terrible messages — some of them racist, some of them asking for money — on various newsgroups throughout the Net. Gerry soon discovered that he was not the only victim that day. Another 200 people in Pennsylvania also had their pass-words cracked! When someone uses your identity on the Net to do something malicious there's not much you can do about it. Except to say: "Don't blame, er, *flame* me."

# Reality Byte

Call them the S.W.A.T team of the Internet. Members of the Forum of Incident Response and Security Team, or FIRST, are the clean-up crew for worms, viruses, and other "sickening" intruders on the Net. You can help them out by being careful about disks and files you put into your computer.

# Sick Computers, Sick Net

Getting sick is no fun for anybody. But it's really no fun when your computer and millions of others get sick at the same time. One of the worst things that can happen on the Net is for your computer to catch a computer virus — a malicious program designed to harm computers and programs. Viruses invade and attach themselves to healthy programs in healthy computers. You usually "catch" a virus by putting something new into your computer: putting a disk in your drive that comes from a contaminated computer; or downloading a contaminated file from the Net through FTP. Or you might hook up to a whole network of computers that has already caught a contagious "bug." Many people have special software to scan or check for viruses on their systems and on disks they put in their disk drives. These virus-checking programs are helpful — and very important to have — but they won't recognize every computer virus in the world. That's because new viruses are being created every day by people who want to harm the Net.

# The Morris Worm

On November 2, 1988, Robert Morris, Jr., created a "worm" that brought 6000 computers on the Net to a standstill. He created a worm-like program that he thought would visit each computer once. The worm crawled from a computer at Cornell University in New York State to other computers across the country. But a programming error meant that the worm kept reinfecting infected computers and kept spreading across the Net until — only a few hours later — part of the Internet's backbone line was all clogged up. The result? A major traffic jam on the I-Way! By the time a computer was cleared of the worm, it was already reinfected and spreading the worm again. So programming teams had to work around the clock for days to stop the Morris worm from crawling around the Net. Morris originally created his worm to test how much damage a worm could cause on the Net and what was needed to stop a worm dead in its tracks. He sure found out, didn't he?

# Computer Doctors to the Rescue!

In the computer world there are expert "doctors" whose job it is to make sick computers better. These people develop programs to de-program the virus programs. The only cure for a virus that's programmed to do harm is another program that's programmed to do some good. But, just like all doctors, computer doctors say that prevention is the best medicine. Their advice to you is this: don't swap disks or download files unless you're absolutely sure that they're not contaminated. Aaa-choo! Bless you.

## Pranking the Net

For some people on the Net every day is April Fool's — time for pranks, jokes, and fake news on the I-Way! Be skeptical about what you read on the Net, and try not to "get had."

**Interplanetary Surfing**
In 1993, Olivier M.J. Crepin-Leblond posted a notice saying that other planets had joined the Internet. He said that new planetary addresses would be identified by these abbreviations: *.ma* for Mars, *.ju* for Jupiter, and *.sa* for Saturn. Most people saw right away that this was a far-out idea!

**Coffee Break**
In 1992, a net user named Brian Kendig posted the following message: ". . . Apple Computer, Inc., made a major addition to the software that runs the Macintosh computer today with the release of Caffeine Manager, an extension that allows all Macintosh computers to interface directly with their coffee percolators and soda machines . . . " Some readers actually called Apple headquarters asking for more information!

**Pigeon Express**
Here's a good one. In 1990, David Waitzman posted a message telling users that carrier pigeons could now be used to transmit Internet messages. He even added detailed technical specifications for what he called the "Transmission of IP Datagrams on Avian Carriers."

# CYBERSTORY

*Tsutomu Shimomura proved that cyberdetectives use the same qualities as other crime fighters: quick thinking and persistence.*

*Notorious hacker Kevin Mitnick broke into computers to steal files and credit card numbers.*

## TRACKING THE HACKER

There's crime on the Net, just like in real life. So cyberdetectives have their work cut out for them, investigating cybercriminals. Here's a story from the Net files.

## December 25, 1994: San Diego, California

Tsutomu Shimomura, one of the world's leading computer-security experts, was shocked and amazed when he realized that a hacker had broken into his home computer and had stolen hundreds of files and software programs. Shimomura decided to track down the criminal.

## One month later: Sausalito, California

Shimomura found out from his friends on the Net that someone had suddenly taken up hundreds of millions of bytes of storage space on a computer server in Sausalito, California. Shimomura checked out the files and found that they were his — the hacker had broken into the server and dumped in Shimomura's files. Shimomura set up a surveillance team to monitor the activities of the intruder. He began to see a pattern he recognized: it looked like the work of Kevin Mitnick, a well-known hacker.

MINNEAPOLIS

SAUSALITO

SAN JOSE

DENVER

SAN DIEGO

RALEIGH

# One week later:
# San Jose, California

The surveillance team moved their headquarters to San Jose because it seemed that
the hacker's service provider was located there. Shimomura discovered
that the hacker's modem was actually calling from three different
places: Denver, Colorado; Minneapolis, Minnesota; and Raleigh, North
Carolina. Hmm . . . very puzzling. Shimomura called in government
investigators and together they pinned down one location: Raleigh,
North Carolina. The hacker was using a telephone switching system
based there. Shimomura hopped on a plane and headed for Raleigh.

# One week later:
# Raleigh, North Carolina

Shimomura drove through the streets of Raleigh with a cellular-phone
technician in his car and a frequency-detecting antenna linked to a
laptop computer. This high-tech search eventually got a signal: it was
coming from Kevin Mitnick's apartment.

# The next day:
# The hacker is caught

Shimomura called in the FBI and they headed over to Mitnick's place.
The authorities entered Mitnick's apartment and found the guilty hacker
hunched over his computer. He was searching for something on the Net.

Kevin Mitnick, age 31, was arrested in February, 1995. He was charged
with stealing $1 million worth of data and 20,000 credit card numbers
through the Internet.

# What's Next on the Net?

The Net is already quite amazing, but every day it gets bigger, faster, and better. How? Thousands of experts all over the world are working on it. And while I-Way construction crews are busy doing their stuff, you just buckle your seatbelt and hang on tight. Next stop, the future!

## High-Speed Hook Ups

As more and more phone lines are being installed around the world — in developing countries and remote areas — more people will be able to hop onto the Net. Experts predict that future Net users will be able to send and receive information — voice, video, and data — much faster than we do now. One high-tech system, called Asynchronous Transfer Mode (ATM), is a way for telephone and digital cable companies to transfer data from analog to digital at high speeds. Through ATM, 10 gigabytes of data — equal to 1000 copies of Webster's dictionary — can be transmitted each second.

## Net Potatoes

Soon your computer may become the one-stop-shop for almost everything you need to see, read, play, buy, or do. The Net can already get you endless amounts of information, and soon you'll be able to hear and see movies and shows on your computer just as clearly as you can on your TV. How? Experts say that someday soon your computer may be plugged into your TV. If this happens, you'll be able to hang out on the couch and "channel" surf the Net. Hey couch potatoes, move over!

## Seeing Is Believing

One day soon you may be able to send "face-mail" instead of e-mail! Video-conferencing, or being able to see and hear the person you are chatting with on your computer screen, is not such a far-off idea. A computer program already exists that lets up to eight Net users see and hear each other at the same time. It's called CU-SeeMe, and some kids have already given it a try. They attended a "classroom" discussion without a classroom, using CU-SeeMe to link a class of kids from all over the world. You can check out this in-your-face technology yourself — just hit Hot Stuff on your Cyber Blastoff disk to get the scoop on how to look your cyberpals straight in the eye!

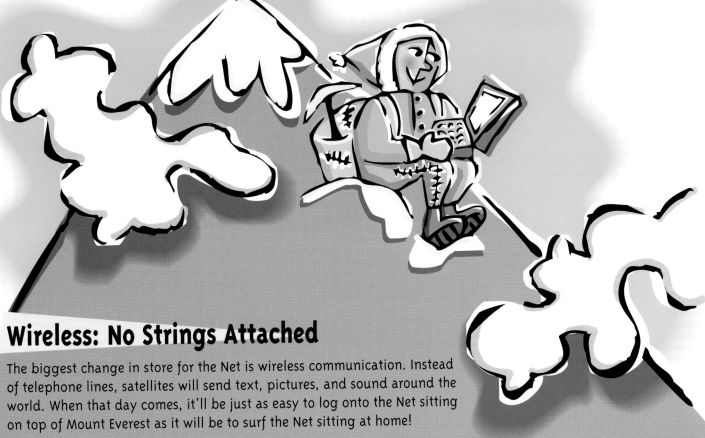

## Wireless: No Strings Attached

The biggest change in store for the Net is wireless communication. Instead of telephone lines, satellites will send text, pictures, and sound around the world. When that day comes, it'll be just as easy to log onto the Net sitting on top of Mount Everest as it will be to surf the Net sitting at home!

# CyberSpeak — A Glossary of Net Words

**analog:** an electronic signal that travels in waves; compare with *digital*

**Archie:** a program on the Net that keeps track of files found in FTP sites

**binary code:** a digital language that is made up of only two characters: on and off, or one and zero

**browser:** a software program that lets you "surf" through the Internet

**central processing unit (CPU):** the part of a computer that controls everything the computer does

**compression program:** a computer program that lets you shrink files so that they take up less space and later expand them back to their original size

**computer:** a digital device that can process data and store it in its "memory"

**crack:** to figure out someone's password or other code for criminal purposes

**cyberspace:** the place where computers "talk" to each other on the Net

**digital:** an electronic signal, used by all computers, made up of binary code; compare with *analog*

**domain:** the last part of an e-mail address describing the kind of user at the address

**downloading:** copying a file of data "down" from one computer and "loading" it onto your own

**e-mail:** electronic mail sent and received by computers

**emoticons:** symbols, made of punctuation marks and letters, that look like facial expressions; also called "smileys"

**File Transfer Protocol (FTP) sites:** databanks on the Net where files of information are available to be downloaded

**flame:** "Net punishment" for someone who has behaved badly on the Net

**freeware:** software that can be downloaded or shared without cost

**Gopher:** a system of programs that list files by topic, and present them on menus

**hacker:** an expert and lawless Net user

**Home Page:** the first screens or "welcome center" of a Web site

**host:** a computer that other computers hook up to so that they can get on the Net

**hypertext:** words at a Web site that appear underlined or in color. By clicking on these words, you "go" to another page or Web site where related information is found

**icons:** pictures on your screen that you click on to give your computer commands

**Information Superhighway:** or I-Way, for short. All the data, video, and voice signals on "roads" made up of telephone lines, digital cables, and satellite signals. Includes the Internet and the World Wide Web.

**input device:** anything — a keyboard, mouse, or joystick — that lets you command your computer

**Internet:** or Net, for short. A worldwide network of computer networks.

**Internet Protocol (IP):** language used by computers to talk to each other. Internet addresses have to meet IP standards to function on the Net.

**Internet Relay Chat (IRC):** when people "talk" to each other on the Net by typing, instead of speaking

**lurker:** someone who listens to an IRC chat but does not join in

**menu:** a list of options

**modem:** or modulator-demodulator. A device that lets computers send and receive digital information across phone lines to and from other computers on the Net

**monitor:** a computer screen

**mouse:** an input device that lets you electronically point to and click on items on your computer screen to give commands

**netiquette:** correct manners and behavior for the Net

**network:** several computers that are linked and can "talk" to each other

**newbie:** a new user on the Internet

**newsgroups:** places where people "chat" on the Net about many different things

**online:** the state of communicating on the Net, between computers, via telephone, satellite, or cable systems

**optical fibers:** high-speed communication cables made of thin strands of glass

**packet:** a small part of a message sent electronically

**password:** a secret combination of letters or numbers, or both, that lets you get your computer on the Net

**protocol:** a system of standards that lets computers interact with each other

**satellite:** a communication device orbiting in space that transmits and receives signals

**satellite dish:** a dish-like antenna on Earth that sends signals to satellites and receives signals bounced back from satellites

**search engine:** a computer program that finds something on the Net for you

**server:** a host computer

**service providers:** companies that you pay so that you can use their servers to access the Net

**shareware:** software that can be downloaded from the Net or another source. If you find it useful, the developer expects to be paid a nominal fee.

**smileys:** symbols, made of punctuation marks and letters, that look like facial expressions

**subdomain:** the part of an e-mail address that is the geographic locator

**surfing:** looking for and finding digital information on the Net

**telephone cable:** one or more pairs of twisted copper wires that carry voice or data as analog signals

**Transmission Control Protocol/Internet Protocol (TCP/IP):** a set of communication standards used to set up the Internet. All networks linked to the Internet use TCP/IP.

**Uniform Resource Locator (URL):** an address for a site on the Web

**Usenet:** where newsgroups and electronic mailing lists are on the Net

**user:** a computer connected to a host computer, and therefore on the Net. Each user is identified by an e-mail address.

**Veronica:** a search engine that searches all the Gopher sites

**virus:** a computer program that "contaminates" computers on the Net and makes them "sick"

**Web site:** a place on the World Wide Web where information, pictures, and other data are available to anyone on the Net

**World Wide Web (WWW):** a part of the Net that uses graphics and hypertext to let you point and click to go to different sites

# Index

# Answers

**Famous First Words,** p. 8:
1., D; 2., E; 3., B; 4., A; 5., C.

**Binary Babble,** p. 15:
GET SET FOR THE NET!

**Cyberjam,** p. 18:
kid **a**'s computer is not hooked up to modem, and keyboard is not hooked up to CPU; kid **b** is all hooked up; kid **c**'s phone is not hooked up to modem; kid **d**'s keyboard is not hooked up to CPU; kid **e** has no modem.

**Name the Domain Game,** p. 23: **C**

**"I Hear Ya!"** p. 27:
Only Basil went to see *Adrenal Pump* with Joshua.

**Talk the Talk,** p. 34:
1, **k**; 2, **c**; 3, **i**; 4, **o**; 5, **a**; 6, **l**; 7, **j**; 8, **m**; 9, **b**; 10, **e**; 11, **d**; 12, **g**; 13, **h**; 14, **n**; 15, **f**.

# Notes to Adults

## On Choosing a Service Provider

Getting online and into cyberspace need not be stressful: there is information available in books and online to help you. The type of Internet access you choose will depend on how much time you will spend online, how much support you will need, and how much money you want to spend. Consider **free access**, through Freenet or at a school or local library. Schools and libraries might levy a small charge for time online, but it will be much less than what you pay a service provider. **Commercial online services**, like Compuserve or America Online, are the most expensive way to surf, but include additional services, such as a Web browser, e-mail, FTP, newsgroups, mailing lists, newspapers and magazines online, bulletin boards, forums, discussion groups, downloadable files, etc. **Internet service providers** — which usually supply a Web browser, e-mail, and a few other services — are less expensive and more basic. There is less online support, but most of the services that aren't offered are available somewhere on the Internet. Ask yourself the following questions:

- What is the dial speed supported by the service provider — 9.6 Kb, 14.4 Kb, 28.8 Kb? The higher the speed the better for faster downloading. At the time of this book's publication, most service providers support a dial speed of 28.8 Kb.
- How much time will I be spending online? Service providers contract for a certain number of hours per day or month, and then charge an hourly rate for use above that rate.
- What is the contention rate — the number of accounts sold per port? If the contention rate is too high, you'll get a busy signal more often when you try to get access to the Internet. A contention rate of 15:1 — 25:1 is acceptable.
- What extras does the service include: an e-mail account, newsfeed, parking for Web pages?
- Do I need support, like help with configuring my machine for access?
- Do I want to use a commercial online service for the support until I am more comfortable online, and then switch to a less expensive Internet service provider?
- Am I taking into account any hidden costs? Things like installation charges, long distance phone rates if your service provider is not local, and hours online beyond the contracted amount could end up costing you unexpectedly.
- Should I consider adding another phone line to my household service? The time my family spends online will tie up the phone line.

## On Safety on the Net for Kids

As a parent or teacher, you want to make sure your kids are as safe when they're online as they are when they're out to play. In addition to our suggestions for street-smart surfing on page 47, warnings about people who might tempt kids to meet them (the offer of expensive computer games for free is pretty irresistible to a kid) should be underlined by you. There are sites specifically set up with information and activities to help you and your kids surf safely. Here's one to check out:

http://www.crc.ricoh.com/people/steve/parents.html

This Net Safety and Censorship site provides parents with lots of information on how kids can use the Net safely: hotlinks to safety sites for kids, links to safety software, and more.

## On Responsible Use of Electronic Media

Like any activity that kids find fun, surfing the Net can be addictive. Just as you are aware of how much TV your kids watch and what they watch, you should stay on top of how much time your kids are spending online and what they are being exposed to there. Your child's unregulated use of the Internet could turn a CyberSurfer into a cyberaddict, and could cost you more money than you want to spend. Setting a schedule and a budget with your kids is a sensible idea.

# CyberSurfer

## "Yellow Pages" Directory

# Let your mouse do the surfing . . .

### Surf Watch

Cyberspace is one hoppin' and happenin' place. So much is going on, it's impossible to keep track of it all! Every day existing sites change, new sites go up, old ones come down, and busy sites move to larger homes. So don't be surprised if some of the sites in these yellow pages look radically different, move to new Net digs or disappear altogether. You can use a search engine to track down those that have moved and lots of cool new sites, too. Along the way, you may hit some "uncool" places on the Net, so just grab your mouse and "click outta there." Plunge in and ride the wave!

### Cyber Blastoff

Most of the more than 250 listings on the following yellow pages are also on the Cyber Blastoff disk that comes with this book. You can use the disk with any Net browser, and it lets you use each listing as a link to the site — you just click on the name of the site to get there. If you are going to surf the Net from the listings here in the book, remember to type the addresses into your computer character for character, all on one line, and without any spaces. The listings are divided into the following subject areas. And don't forget to keep an eye out for Cyberstops — neat sites just for fun!

Animals
Ask an Expert
Books 'n' Stuff
Cyberkids in Action
Dinosaurs
Environment
Games, Puzzles 'n' Fun
Geography

Government
History
Insects
International Kids Pages
K.O.O.L. — Kids Only OnLine
Math
Movies
Museums
Music

Schools on the Net
Science
Space
Sports
The Tube — TV
Virtual References
Visual Arts
The "Write" Stuff

# Surfers' Legend of Sights and Sounds

**C**   Chat with other kids here.

**DF**   Download cool files here.

**HL**   Find hotlinks to cool sites here.

**M**   Watch QuickTime movies or videos here, if you have a movie-player program installed on your computer.

**P**   View photos here.

**S**   Listen to music or messages here, if you have a sound application program on your computer. (If your computer is an IBM, you'll need speakers, too.)

**AOL**   America Online Kids Only (available only to subscribers)

**PRO**   Prodigy (available only to subscribers)

## ANIMALS

### Animals Around the World   HL
http://www.chicojr.chico.k12.ca.us/staff/gray/animals.html

Welcome to animal hotlink central. This Web page is crammed with urls for all kinds of animals: bears, wolves, caribou, otters, alligators, llamas, wombats, cats, dogs, dolphins, jellyfish, corals, penguins . . . . Grab your mouse and start surfing!

### The Buzbee Bat House Temperature Plot   HL P
http://nyx10.cs.du.edu:8001/~jbuzbee/bat_house.html

"Holy bat box, Batman! It's the Buzbee Bat House!" One of the most important things that bats look for when they choose a place to roost is its temperature. Check out this graph of the temperature inside a bat house, and drive your mouse batty by surfing the hotlinks!

### Charlotte, The Vermont Whale   P
http://www.uvm.edu/whale/TableOfContents.html

Could a whale swim to Vermont? You bet it could — if it was a prehistoric whale! Find out how Charlotte the beluga whale got to inland Vermont, how nature preserved her bones until they were discovered in 1849, and what this discovery means to scientists today.

### The Electronic Zoo   HL M P S
http://netvet.wustl.edu/e-zoo.htm

The Electronic Zoo has got lots of byte. Bytes of information that is! The zoo is hotwired to lots of animal resources around the Net — FTP, Gopher, World Wide Web sites, and newsgroups. It's also a great place to find animal photos and sounds.

### Elephant — Facts at Your Fingertips
http://www.the-body-shop.com/ele.html#eia

Get the hard and fast facts on one of the world's largest and most endangered animals. Zip into this site and find out what people around the world are doing to save elephants and what you can do, too.

### Endangered Species of Canada
http://www.ncf.carleton.ca/freenet/rootdir/menus/social.services/eco/gorgs/cc-biodiv/files/species

If you want the facts and nothing but the facts on some of Canada's endangered species — sea otters, leatherback turtles, beluga whales, whooping cranes, and cougars to name a few — then point your mouse in this direction.

### The Great White Shark   HL P
http://ucmp1.berkeley.edu/Doug/shark.html

Jump into the Net surf with the great white shark — if you dare. At this site, graduate student Douglas Long explains how researchers study sharks and how they go about identifying individual sharks. You'll also find some great underwater shots of these fearsome predators. Jaws, anyone?

### Hinterland Who's Who   HL P S
http://www.doe.ca:80/envcan/eng_ind.html

Here's a fab online index of the who's who of Canadian wildlife. Find out about the habitat, habits, life history, and physical characteristics of loons, snowy owls, beavers, woodchucks, and lots of other Canuck critters. Click away!

### Kids' Action: Rainforest Animals   P
http://www.ran.org/ran/kids_action/animals.html

More than half of all the known species in the world live in tropical rainforests. No kidding! Gorillas, jaguars, toucans, parrots, and tarantulas, to name a few. Here you'll find out why so many animals live in rainforests, how they manage to live together, how some are becoming extinct, neat animal facts, and more!

### Mad About Marmosets   P
http://loki.ur.utk.edu/ut2kids/primates/marmosets.html

Dr. Suzette Tardif is mad about marmosets. In fact, she's been studying these monkey-like creatures that live in South American jungles for most of her life! Not much is known about these mysterious animals. In this hypertext story, Tardif talks about her research and the little information that we do have.

### PetStation Kids!   C HL P
http://petstation.com/kids.html

Stop at the PetStation and visit the Bird Barn, Cat Cabana, Dog Domain, Fish Fair, Herp Hacienda (amphibians and reptiles), Horse Heaven, Small Mammal Medley, and more. You'll find photos, articles, and tips on your favorite pets. This site is also a great place to meet cyberpals from around the world.

### The Raptor Center   P S
http://www.raptor.cvm.umn.edu/

No, this is not a center for the velociraptors of Jurassic Park. Here, the word "raptor" means a bird of prey such as an owl, falcon, or eagle. The center's mission is to protect and preserve these birds. This site has some cool raptor sights and sounds as well as a raptor fact Gopher that will hold your rapt attention.

### Rhinos and Tigers and Bears — Oh My!   P
http://loki.ur.utk.edu/ut2kids/zoo/zoo.html

What's a baby rhino doing with a bowling ball? A tiger with a barrel? And a bear with a plastic pipe? Playing! In this hypertext article, read about these zoo "animal enrichment" activities and find out what it takes to become a zoologist.

### SeaWorld and Busch Gardens   M P S
http://www.bev.net/education/SeaWorld/homepage.html

This site is just loaded with cool info about animals. You can look through the Animal Bytes for fast and fun facts and then scan the animal information database for more details. Try the animal sound quiz in which you match sounds with the animals that make them. And if you've got a question about the ocean or marine mammals, you can e-mail it to Ask Shamu.

### Whale Watching Web   HL P S
http://www.physics.helsinki.fi/whale/

For a whale of a time, cruise over to this site in Helsinki, Finland. Here you can get the lowdown on whale watching around the world, check out cool whale songs and pics, and ride hotlinks to other whale sites on the Net.

## Wolves on the Web  HL P S

http://wwwnncc.scs.unr.edu/wolves/desertm.html

This site will make you howl at the moon. It's jam-packed with tons of hotlinks to wolf information on the Net, wolf pics and sounds, and way more. Arrrooooo!

## World Wildlife Fund  P

http://www.envirolink.org/orgs/wqed/wwf/wwf_home.html

The World Wildlife Fund is working to preserve plants and animals around the world. Check out their global field notes and news blasts. Go wild!

## Zoo Atlanta Home Page  DF HL M P S

http://www.gatech.edu/3020/zoo/home-page.html

Download these animal sights, sounds, and action clips and you'll be in a virtual zoo all of your own! Photos of cheetahs, zebras, and tree frogs, sounds of kookaburras, crows, and rattlesnakes, and movies of turtles, giraffes, and killer whales are just a few of the goodies you'll find here.

## ZooNet  HL P

http://www.mindspring.com/~zoonet/

ZooNet links up zoos around the world. Check out its animal photo archives and surf its hotlinks to zoos and animal home pages all around the world!

## ASK AN EXPERT

### Ask Beth  PRO
Jump: ASK BETH

Need some advice about something personal? A really embarrassing situation? Your family? Your friends? Just ask Beth. Beth (Elizabeth Winship) is the *Boston Globe*'s advice columnist for teenagers and parents. She's prepared to handle "the tough stuff."

### Ask Betty the Bug Lady  HL P S

http://www.nj.com/yucky/betty/index.html

When Dr. Betty Faber was a kid, she was completely terrified of flying cockroaches — and completely fascinated by them. Today she's an insect expert, or entomologist, and a bona fide authority on cockroaches. Send her your buggy questions here.

### Ask Dr. Math

http://forum.swarthmore.edu/dr.math/dr-math.html

Stumped by a mind-boggling math question? Search through Dr. Math's archives for expertly explained solutions to similar problems. And if all else fails, e-mail it to the Swat Team at Ask Dr. Math. They'll deboggle it and send you a step-by-step solution. Swat that!

### Ask-a-Geologist

http://walrus.wr.usgs.gov/docs/ask-a-ge.html

Ever wondered if mountains are growing? If scientists can predict earthquakes? Or what makes a volcano erupt? Now you can e-mail your questions about earth sciences to Ask-a-Geologist and have a real geologist answer them for you.

## Ask Shamu

http://www.bev.net/education/SeaWorld/ask_shamu/asintro.html

Do dolphins have larger brains than humans? What was the largest tidal wave ever recorded? How do you train whales and dolphins? Scroll through the Ask Shamu Index to find the answers to these questions and others asked by kids. And if you've got your own burning question about the ocean or marine animals, e-mail it to Ask Shamu!

## Ask a Volcanologist  HL P

http://volcano.und.nodak.edu/vwdocs/ask_a.html

If a red-hot question about volcanoes is erupting in your brain, this is the place to spew it. But take a look through the previously asked questions first to make sure your question hasn't already been answered. After you've fired off your question, take the hotlink to Volcano World. Lava rules!

## Ask the Harkster  P

http://www.nais.ccm.emr.ca/schoolnet/harkster/Home.html

Got a question about Canadian geography? Send it to the Harkster — the master of Canadian Geography. "Nobody has ever stumped the Harkster" — yet. E-mail away!

## How's the Weather, Harold?  P S

http://sln.fi.edu/franklin/scientst/harold.html

Ask Harold Vanasse, the chief meteorologist of the Franklin Institute, how the weather is and he won't dodge the question. But he won't guarantee his answer either! Predicting the weather is like trying to predict the unpredictable. You can e-mail questions and messages to Harold and test out the site's weather forecaster to forecast the weather for your hometown!

## Jumble and Crossword Solver

http://odin.chemistry.uakron.edu/cbower/jumble.html

Got a pesky jumbled word that you just can't unscramble or a crossword puzzle that refuses to be solved? Then drop by this site and put a computer on the job. Enter the scrambled word (or letter clues) and the computer will generate a list of all the possible words the word could be. The word list is linked to Webster's online dictionary, so you can look up any words that you don't know to see if they match the clues. Whew!

## On-line Writing Lab Grammar Hotline

http://athena.english.vt.edu/owl_www/owl.html

If you've got a question about writing or a finicky query about grammar, e-mail it to the grammar busters at Virginia Tech's Writing Center. They'll try to get back to you as soon as possible. Write on!

## TIME for Kids — Ask an Editor  AOL
Go to BRAIN FUEL

Here's a direct line to TIME Magazine's editors, reporters, writers, researchers, and correspondents. They all hang out on this bulletin board and they'll answer your questions personally. So ask away!

◆ ◆ ◆ ◆ ◆ ◆ ◆ ◆ ◆ ◆ ◆ ◆

## CYBERSTOP

### The Electric Postcard

http://postcards.www.media.mit.edu/Postcards/

Want to drop your cyberpals a line about a way cool site you've just discovered? Or tell your family some of your cybersurfing stories? Or just say "Hello"? Send them a postcard from the Electric Postcard. There are lots of neat cards to choose from. E-mail away!

◆ ◆ ◆ ◆ ◆ ◆ ◆ ◆ ◆ ◆ ◆ ◆

## BOOKS 'N' STUFF

### Children's Literature Web Guide  HL

http://www.ucalgary.ca/~dkbrown/index.html

Here's an awesome guide to kid lit — literature, that is — on the Net. Use it to find online stories and books, kids' writing, and online markets for your own writing. Get clicking!

### The Comic Strip

http://www.unitedmedia.com/comics/

Get your smiles and chuckles here! Check out some of your fab comix faves: Marmaduke, the Born Loser, Dilbert, Robotman, Dr. Fun — the first comic strip ever created just for the Net — and more. And if you've ever wanted to be a cartoonist, click through Dilbert: A Day in the Life of cartoonist Scott Adams.

### CRAYON — CreAte Your Own Newspaper  HL

http://sun.bucknell.edu/~boulter/crayon/

Color your world with CRAYON by CreAting Your Own Newspaper! Pick and choose the kinds of news, comic strips, and the like that you want to read everyday and put together your own personal newspaper. It'll be updated daily — CRAYON keeps you current!

### International Student Newswire  HL

http://www.umassd.edu/SpecialPrograms/ISN/KidNews.html

Hungry for some news? Park your mouse at this international news service for students and teachers and click through news bytes, sports bytes, feature stories, people stories, how-to stories, and reviews written by kids. Send your own stories to Newswire, too!

### MidLink Magazine  HL P

http://longwood.cs.ucf.edu:80/~MidLink/

This radical e-zine links 10- to 15-year-old kids around the world. Each cyberissue is crammed with lots of fun stuff: kids' art, laugh links, the "write" spot to submit your own writing, virtual tours, and more. MidLink also hooks up to scientific projects where you can ask real scientists questions. It's a way cool read!

### Online Book Initiative Gopher DF P

gopher://ftp.std.com:70/11/obi/

Looking for a good book to read? Gopher one here and download it! The Online Book Initiative is packed with fairy tales, the adventures of detective Sherlock Holmes, E. Nesbit's *The Five Children and It*, and way, way more!

### OWL Kids Online HL P S

http://www.owl.on.ca

Swoop in to one of the funkiest sites on the Net. Check out way cool science and nature stuff and more from OWL Magazine, Owl Books, and Owl/TV. E-mail your favorite jokes and Web sites to OWL — they want to hear from you!

### Project Gutenberg Home Page DF

http://jg.cso.uiuc.edu/pg/pg_home.html

Back in the 1400s, Johann Gutenberg invented the printing press, which made it possible to produce books for the masses. Today the Gutenberg Project has created a "Net press." By entering books in the public domain into a computer, the Gutenberg Project is making it possible "for everyone in the world to have a copy." Check out popular classics such as *Anne of Green Gables*, *Tom Sawyer*, *Huckleberry Finn*, *Alice in Wonderland*, and many more.

### Radio Aahs Online M P S

http://www.radio-aahs.com

Radio Aahs, the kids' 24-hour radio network, blasts the cyberwaves! This site is packed with lots of cool stuff: late-breaking news, puzzles and fun, kids' heroes, top-10 lists, interviews with stars, and reviews of books, movies, CDs, and video games. There's even a place where you can ask for advice about tough problems or questions — aaaahht last!

### Sports Illustrated for Kids Online P

http://www.pathfinder.com/@@WqCNLgAAAAA AADAK/SIFK/index.html

Sports Illustrated for Kids Online is loaded with lots of neat stuff. Check out the articles and facts on world-class athletes, athletes that share your birthday, kids' art and stories, sports tips, and the SI for Kids Challenge. Surf on in, dude!

### TIME for Kids P

http://www.pathfinder.com/@@fz80kgAAAAAAA DQK/TFK/

TIME's team of correspondents around the world file "up-to-the-minute" stories each week in this version of TIME for Kids. Find out about current events, new books and movies, kids who are making headlines, and lots more. TIME really does fly!

### Explore PathFinder HL P

http://www.pathfinder.com/@@bNBvTAAAAAAA AHQB/pathfinder/explore.html

Step into another dimension: the TIME Warner online universe. It's the home of Encyclopedia Britannica Online and TIME, Life, People, Entertainment Weekly, and lots of other e-zines. Head for Kidstuff and click your way into Radio Aahs' e-zine, Sports Illustrated for Kids, and TIME for Kids. Choose your own path!

### Twisted Tales PRO

Jump: TWISTED TALES

If you want to read (and write!) stories that are totally twisted (as twisted as your brain can twist 'em), then this is the place to go. Key in the words you're asked for and the story will literally write, er, twist itself onto your screen. Mind warp!

## CYBERKIDS IN ACTION

### Ben Nelson's Fantastic Web!! HL P

http://netaccess.on.ca/~bnelson/index.html

Thirteen-year-old Ben Nelson has a fantastic (incredible, beautiful, fantastically well made) home page (see p. 35). But don't take our word for it. Check it out for yourself. Explore weird links, dead-end links, and some funky games created by Ben himself.

### CitySpace M P

http://cityspace.org/

CitySpace is a three-dimensional virtual city that kids built together on the Net (see p. 29). Find out about this cool project here and meet some of the kids who participated. Surf on in!

### The Computer Clubhouse @ The Computer Museum P

http://www.net.org/clubhouse/index.html

This is one wired clubhouse! The kids who hang out here use computers to develop their own projects. Some of them are using the World Wide Web to build their family trees. The Clubhouse has also created an online art gallery. Drop by and see what these kids are up to!

### CyberKids DF HL

http://www.woodwind.com/mtlake/CyberKids/ CyberKids.html

Click your way through this nifty magazine published by kids for other kids on the Net. If you've got a story idea or some art you'd like to see published in the magazine, Cyberkids wants to hear from you. It's a great place to find cyber-pals, too.

### The CyberSpace Middle School HL P

http://www.scri.fsu.edu/~dennisl/CMS.html

The CyberSpace Middle School is "not just a school, but an adventure." Here you can ride a virtual school bus around the Net, read about the school's special projects, and surf their hotlinks to cool places on the Web. Going to school was never so much fun!

### Hillside Elementary School M P

http://hillside.coled.umn.edu/

These amazing Web pages have been created by the kids at Hillside Elementary School in Minnesota. And they've packed them with lots of radical stuff. Read the Buzz Rod story and choose your own ending. (There are 22 endings in all!) Check out the kids' projects and book reviews, too.

### Kids Did This! Hotlist HL

http://sln.fi.edu/tfi/hotlists/kids.html#physical

On the Net, kids rule. Just check out this hotlist of awesome Internet projects kids have done in science, art, history, math, and language arts. Cool stuff!

### By Kids ... For Kids P

http://riceinfo.rice.edu/armadillo/Rice/ Students/bykid2.html

By Kids ... For Kids is a newsletter for kids in fourth grade completely edited, written, and published by fourth graders Zach Edgerton and Sam Bryan. Check it out!

### MayaQuest Learning Adventure DF HL P

http://mayaquest.mecc.com/

The ancient Mayan civilization built huge pyramids in Mexico and Central America around 250 AD. In 1995 the MayaQuest cycling expedition (see p. 42) set out on bicycles to investigate why the Mayan civilization crumbled, and thousands of kids around the world tracked them through the Net. This site tells the story of the MayaQuest adventure. Pedal on in!

### VidKids M P S

http://cmp1.ucr.edu/exhibitions/cmp_ed_prog.h tml

The VidKids did what? Made their own videos? Wow! Meet the VidKids, students in grades one to four, and check out their cool photo and video projects. E-mail them your comments — they want to hear from you!

◆ ◆ ◆ ◆ ◆ ◆ ◆ ◆ ◆ ◆ ◆

## CYBERSTOP

### The Internet Pizza Server Home Page

http://www.ecst.csuchico.edu/~pizza/

Got the cybersurfin' munchies? How about a fresh slice of cyberpizza? This is where you can order virtual pizza that's really out of this world!

◆ ◆ ◆ ◆ ◆ ◆ ◆ ◆ ◆ ◆ ◆

## DINOSAURS

### Dinosaur Antechamber P

http://ucmp1.berkeley.edu/expo/cladecham. html

Step into this virtual antechamber, or waiting room, and take a good look at some of your favorite dinosaurs, T Rex for one. Check out their body structure, what they ate, and how they lived from day to day. It's dino-mite!

### Dilophosaurus! A Narrated Exhibition HL P S

http://ucmp1.berkeley.edu/dilophosaur/intro. html

Meet Dilophosaurus — a dinosaur with a thumb much like yours! Professor Sam Welles describes how he and a team paleontologists discovered this double-crested dinosaur and pieced together the details of its life. The professor also debunks the image of Dilophosaurus in Jurassic Park.

### DNA to Dinosaurs Project  M P S
http://rs6000.bvis.uic.edu:80/museum/exhibits/Exhibits.html

Follow the footprints on your screen to travel millions of years back in time on this virtual tour of life from DNA to dinosaurs. Dial 1-900-CLIMATE for the Triassic period forecast and check out animated movies of dinosaurs on the run. This is one of the best dino sites on the Web!

### Honolulu Community College Dinosaur Exhibit  HL P S
http://www.hcc.hawaii.edu/dinos/dinos.1.html

Take this narrated virtual dino tour and find out about Triceratops, T Rex, Stegosaurus, Hypelosaurus, Iguanadon, and Deinonychus. And check out the site's hotlinks (just click on Other Internet Resources) to find dino pics and shots from Jurassic Park.

### Movie Dinosaurs
http://ericir.syr.edu/Newton/Lessons/moviedino.html

Just how did they create the dinosaurs in Jurassic Park? The special effects company Industrial Light and Magic had lots of animators, artists, computer programmers, and technicians work on the dinos together. Surf to this site and get the inside scoop on some of their trade secrets.

### Scotty: the Tyrannosaurus Rex at Eastend, Saskatchewan  HL P
http://www.lights.com/scotty/

This site will take you to pictures of what Scotty's head, skull, and leg may have looked like. But the best part of the site has got to be the hot dino links.

### The Palaeontological Institute of the Russian Academy of Science in Moscow, Russia  P
http://ucmp1.berkeley.edu/pin.html

Head into Russia and drop by the largest paleontological institute in the world. Check out the institute's Mongolian dinosaurs, ice-age animals, and ancient mammals. Rush in!

## ENVIRONMENT

### 40 Tips to Go Green
http://www.ncb.gov.sg/jkj/env/greentips.html

These green tips come from the Jalan Hijau environmental action group in Singapore. They're simple, everyday things that you can do to make a difference. Go green!

### Earth Force
gopher://gopher.earthforce.org:7007/

At Earth Force, "kids make it go" and "kids make it grow"! This organization of kids takes action to make an environmental difference and helps kids get information about the environment. Check out some of the cool things these kids are doing!

### EarthKids Hawaii  HL
http://hookomo.aloha.net/epf/dsg/ekh/

Here's where you can find out what Hawaiian kids have to say about the environment. Check out their story page, art gallery, and funky hotlinks, too.

### EcoNet  HL
http://www.econet.apc.org/econet/en.issues.html

EcoNet is a one-stop environmental resource center. It's loaded with hotlinks to information about acid rain, biodiversity, climate, endangered species, energy, environmental law, forests, toxic waste, water, wildlife, and more!

### The Enviro Web  C HL P S
http://envirolink.org/

Touch down at the largest online environmental service on the planet. Click through the virtual environmental library, the enviro arts gallery, the environmental resource directory, and more. This site will lead you to almost anything you're looking for on the environment.

### Environmental Express
http://www.scholastic.com/public/Network/EnviroExpress/Environmental-Express.html

Hop on the Environmental Express and take a look at some artwork, plays, stories, and poems that kids have created to celebrate Earth Day. We've only got one planet!

### Environment Canada
http://www.doe.ca/

Cruise down Canada's green lane on the information highway. Here you can check out hot environmental issues and topics, endangered species, what's happening in the Great Lakes, and the Canadian biodiversity network. You can even send e-mail to Canada's Minister of the Environment!

### International Arctic Project Home Page  P
http://www.scholastic.com/public/Network/IAP/IAP-Home.html

In 1995, a team of international scientists and explorers crossed the Arctic Ocean on dogsleds and canoe-sleds to raise awareness of the Arctic's important role in the Earth's ecosystem. You can find out about this fascinating journey here. Check out the team's reports, maps, bios, dogs, gear, supplies, food, and more.

### Ocean Planet Online  M P
http://seawifs.gsfc.nasa.gov/ocean_planet.html

Plunge into the depths and virtually explore the ocean in this cool online exhibit from the Smithsonian. Watch an undersea flyby, play biological roulette, check out the dangers facing oceans, and much, much more. Ocean Planet Online is one deep site!

### Rainforest Action Network  P
http://www.ran.org/ran/kids_action/index.html

Kids can take action to save the world's rainforests. Here's where you can find out what you can do. Check out animals and people of the rainforest and rainforest questions and answers, too. You've got the power!

### TOPEX/Poseidon Online  DF HL P
http://quest.arc.nasa.gov/topex/welcome.html

TOPEX/Poseidon's mission is to develop and operate a satellite system that observes the ocean. You'll find lots of neat stuff here: images from the satellite, day-in-the-life journals of the people who run the satellite, questions and answers, and more. Take the plunge!

◆ ◆ ◆ ◆ ◆ ◆ ◆ ◆ ◆

## CYBERSTOP

### Virtual Scrabble with the Simpsons  P
http://www.webcom.com/~shanti/scrab.html

Drop in on the Simpsons as they battle wits in a fierce game of Scrabble. Take a look at the last four moves of the game and then suggest a move for your favorite Simpson character to make. Help Bart, Lisa, Marge, and Homer squabble, er, scrabble it out!

◆ ◆ ◆ ◆ ◆ ◆ ◆ ◆ ◆

## GAMES, PUZZLES, 'N' FUN

### Carlos' Coloring Book Home  DF
http://robot0.ge.uiuc.edu/~carlosp/color/

You won't have any problem staying inside the lines of this coloring book. That's because you use your mouse to point and click the color where you want it. Download your picture when you're done. And if your computer's a Macintosh, you can download a coloring program, too.

### The Chess Server
http://www.willamette.edu/~tjones/chessmain.html

Chess anyone? At the Chess Server, you can play chess with players from all around the world. Drop by and sign in or post a note on the bulletin board to tell other players when you'll be dropping by next. It's a great way to check for a chess mate!

### A Collection of 3-D Pictures  DF
http://fmechds01.tu-graz.ac.at/heidrun/3d/3dpic2.html

The whole world's gone dotty! That's what it may seem like when you take a look at these 3-D pics. Try making your own 3-D pics with the cool software you can download here.

### The Games Domain  DF HL
http://www.gamesdomain.co.uk/

Do not pass Go. Do not collect $200. You are about to enter the Games Domain. Here you'll find anything and everything that's related to games: games to download, hints and cheats, game reviews, and lots and lots of hot game links.

## Games on the Internet  DF HL

http://www.misha.net:80/~pup/games/lordsoth/

You've just struck games' gold! This site has hundreds of games for DOS and Windows users to download. And if you find there's just too much to choose from, you can scroll down the top-25 list to narrow down your options. Surfing for games can be a tough life!

## Hangman

http://www.cm.cf.ac.uk/htbin/RobH/hangman

Five strikes and he's hung! This site plays a tough game of Hangman. So if you get really stumped, try the online Jumble and Crossword Solver (see Ask an Expert). But remember to go there in a new window or else you could lose your game.

## LEGO™ Information  DF M P S

http://legowww.homepages.com/

Le'go my LEGO! If you've said that more than once, then this site is a must see. It's got LEGO games, a LEGO theme song, LEGO robots, descriptions and ratings of the latest LEGO sets, and software that lets you create virtual LEGO. For LEGO maniacs only!

## Lite Brite

http://www.galcit.caltech.edu/~ta/lb/lb.html

Light up your life with a little Lite Brite. Create a picture online by clicking on "Edit" and following the directions on screen. When you're done, you can post your masterpiece in the gallery.

## Mac Games for the Downloading  DF

ftp://nic.switch.ch/software/mac/umich-mac-shadow/game

Enter a galaxy of games for kids who have Mac computers. You'll find tons of great adventure, space, word, card, board, and arcade games to download here. But don't let the huge selection send your head for a spin — prepare to get in the game!

## Magic Eye

http://www.magiceye.com/magiceye/

Slip into the Magic Eye's world of 3-D illusions. Check out the 3-D images of the month. Find out how to view the illusions and how they work. There's more to these illusions than meets the eye!

## Mr. Potato Head  M P

http://winnie.acsu.buffalo.edu/potatoe/

On the Net, Mr. Potato Head goes by the name Mr. Edible Starchy Tuber Head. But he's still the same old starchy oddball. Check out this cool site where you can play Mr. Potato Head, watch him fly, and take a look at a potato cam.

## Nintendo  HL

http://www.nintendo.com/

This is the place to get the lowdown on the latest stuff from Nintendo. Check out their upcoming games to find out about new characters, new levels, and hidden stuff. Go on a game adventure, too!

## Optical Illusions

http://www.scri.fsu.edu/~dennisl/topics/optical.html

Bend your brain with the optical illusions at this site. They're opti-cool!

## PC Games for the Downloading  DF

ftp://garbo.uwasa.fi/windows/educgames/

Get set to do some serious downloading. This is a games goldmine for kids who have PCs that run Windows. You'll find board games, card games, brain bogglers, word games, puzzles, and mazes. Not to mention MasterMind, Story Twister, and Tetris. Just how game are you?

## Galaxy of Games  DF PRO

Jump: GAME CENTER

Explore Prodigy's galaxy of games and you'll discover sports games, strategy games, quick games, and humorous games to play as well as game news, hints, and bulletin-board notes. Pro diggity dog!

## Sega Online  HL M P S

http://www.segaoa.com/

Enter Sega's online universe where you can find out about Sega's latest video games, send messages to Sega's game developers, chat live as your favorite Sega character, and lots more. Are you game?

## WWW Spirograph

http://juniper.tc.cornell.edu:8000/spiro/spiro.html

Get set to send your brain for a spin by playing spirograph on the Web. One, two, three — everybody rotate!

## Video Games WWW Sites  HL

http://www.infolink.net/~chimo/smss/html/videowww.html

This site will link you to tons of video game sites around the Net. Look for sites devoted to all your favorite video games. Get clicking!

## Zarf's List of Interactive Games on the Web  HL

http://www.cs.cmu.edu/afs/andrew/org/kgb/www/zarf/games.html

Zap over to Zarf's hotlink heaven! This hotlist is crammed with links to lots of zany interactive games and toys on the Web. Play with an online ouija board, slot machine, and games galore!

# GEOGRAPHY

## April's Antarctic Adventures  P

http://pen1.pen.k12.va.us/~alloyd/AAA.html

Get set to explore Antarctica — the coldest, harshest continent on the planet — with April. Check out extreme cold-weather gear that she has to wear while she's there. Then visit the McMurdo sound research station and don't forget to go boondoggling!

## Asia Cyberspace  HL P

http://silkroute.com/silkroute/asia/rsrc/country/japan.html

Visit the cyberspace country of Japan. Take a look at the collection of Japanese photos, read the traveller's diary of a 1923 journey to Japan in the year of the Great Tokyo Earthquake, and surf the links to Japanese Web servers.

## Ask the Harkster  P

http://www-nais.ccm.emr.ca/schoolnet/harkster/Home.html

Got a question about Canadian geography? Send it to the Harkster — the master of Canadian Geography. "Nobody has ever stumped the Harkster" — yet. E-mail away!

## Blacksburg Electronic Village  HL P

http://www.bev.net/index.html

The Blacksburg Electronic Village links the people who live in Blacksburg to the Net and each other. Check out the local school's home pages and projects. And take the Education Center's hotlinks to Sea World and Busch Gardens' Animal Information Database, an online writing workshop, and other happenin' places around the Net.

## City.Net  P

http://www.city.net/cnx/about_cnx.html

City.Net is one wired world. It's linked up to just about every city in the world that's on the Net. Take a look at maps, photos, and landmarks of foreign cities and countries. Find out about the history and literature of different regions, too. Travel virtually!

## Colour Tour of Egypt  P

http://www.memphis.edu/egypt/egypt.html

Cybersurf your way into this fascinating land of pyramids and ancient pharaohs. Walk along the Nile river, visit the Temple of Isis, and take a hotlink to an exhibition of Egyptian artifacts. Way cool!

## Earth Viewer  DF

http://www.fourmilab.ch/earthview/vplanet.html

Many astronauts say the best part of being in space is looking at the spectacular view of Earth. You may not be able to go up in the shuttle anytime soon, but you can use Earth Viewer to take a look at Earth from the moon, the sun, or a space satellite. Check out the map that shows up-to-date views of the day and night regions of the Earth, too.

### Gateway to Antarctica HL

http://icair.iac.org.nz/

This is definitely one of the coolest places on the Web! Surf through the gateway to find out about Antarctica's environment, wildlife, scientific research projects, and international treaties. Then thumb through the little white book of Antarctic addresses and ride the hotlinks around this icy zone.

### Geographical Gopher P

gopher://cne.gsfc.nasa.gov:70/11/Other%20Resources/Other%20online%20Libraries

If you're looking for information about the Middle East, the former Soviet Union, Africa, Asia, Europe, or South America, just go-pher it! This online library will lead you to facts, photos, maps, and governmental, historical, and cultural info about these far-flung places.

### The Interactive Tour of Tassie P

http://info.utas.edu.au/docs/tastour/tourhome.html

Do Tasmanian devils really exist outside of Bugs Bunny cartoons? You bet they do! These feisty critters are known for their bad temper. Take this virtual tour of Tasmania and you'll discover the island's lush landscape and unique plants and animals. Click on the map and go!

### The Journey North

http://ics.soe.umich.edu/ed712/IAPIntro.html

Come on a virtual journey to the Arctic. Get into the mood by reading poetry, Inuit writings, and newspaper articles. Then follow Arctic wildlife as they head north. You can check out explorers' reports from the 1994 International Arctic Project that studied the Arctic environment and Inuit culture, too.

### Kid's Window on Japan P S

http://kiku.stanford.edu:80/KIDS/kids_home.html

Peek through this virtual window on the unique culture of Japan. Find out about scrumptious Japanese foods, learn how to speak and write in Japanese, and try the Japanese art of paper folding called origami.

### Mapmaker, Mapmaker, Make Me a Map

http://loki.ur.utk.edu/ut2kids/maps/map.html

This cool hypertext article will give you the lowdown on mapmaking. It looks at all sorts of different maps: political maps, physical maps, road maps, and weather maps. Map this site on your hotlist!

### National SchoolNet Atlas

http://www-nais.ccm.emr.ca/schoolnet/

The National SchoolNet Atlas has maps of Canada and the world, facts about Canada, hot topics and issues, and a geographical name search engine. You can also use it to test your knowledge of Canadian geography and to create your own maps. Map a bookmark here!

### Ragu Presents — Mama's Cucina S

http://www.eat.com/

Ragu presents Mama's Cucina (kitchen). Take Italian lessons from Professore Antonio — just click on Italian words and sentences and the Professore teaches you how to say them. Check out Mama's recipes and surf the hotlinks to Web sites in Italy. Mama mia!

### The Virtual Tourist HL

http://wings.buffalo.edu/world/

Cybersurf around the world in 80 virtual days, hours, or seconds! Just click anywhere on this world map and you'll travel there — virtually. Then you can explore the hotlist of regional Internet sites and do some site-seeing. There's no better way to see the world on the Net. Bon voyage, cybersurfer!

### Virtually Hawaii P

http://www.satlab.hawaii.edu/space/hawaii/

Surf into the surfing capital of the world (Hawaiians invented the nifty water sport) and let your mouse go wild. Explore the islands' lava-spitting volcanoes, drive along Chain of Craters Road, climb Mount Haleakala, and check out some aerial and satellite photos, too. Aloha!

### Window-to-Russia Home Page HL P

http://www.kiae.su/www/wtr/

Catch this wave through Russia and click it to the max! Take a tour of the Kremlin, thumb through an interactive English-Russian dictionary, visit a gallery of "hot pictures," meet a Russian cartoonist, and way, way more!

◆ ◆ ◆ ◆ ◆ ◆ ◆ ◆ ◆ ◆

## CYBERSTOP

### Computer Science House Drink Machine P

http://www.csh.rit.edu/proj/drink.html

Surfing sure works up a thirst. Drop by the Computer Science House for a virtual drink. Their pop machines are really wired. They don't accept quarters or any other coins. Members of the House log on their computers to "drop a drink," and then their computerized "credit accounts" are charged. Sounds like they've invented a compopter!

◆ ◆ ◆ ◆ ◆ ◆ ◆ ◆ ◆ ◆

## GOVERNMENT

### The Canadian House of Commons P

http://www.emr.ca/opengov/commons/commons.html

The Canadian House of Commons is anything but common. It's the place where all the important government debates happen! Check out the government in action. Use the map of Canada to find your local Member of Parliament (MP) or check out the MPs in each political party.

### Canada — Open Government HL P S

http://www.emr.ca/opengov/index.html

Think of this site as a central database for the government of Canada. First off, you can listen to the national anthem. Dig a little deeper and you can find out about the Supreme Court of Canada, government departments, important government documents, the federal budget, the political parties, the provincial governments . . . you get the picture.

### Central Intelligence Agency Server HL P S

http://www.odci.gov/cia/

Find out what the CIA's mission really is. Slip into your trench coat and steal into the agency over this direct cyberline. Check out their World Fact Book. It's got maps and important info such as population figures and international conflicts involving just about any country you can name!

### Governments on the Internet HL

http://www.emr.ca/opengov/world.html

Ever wondered what the government is like in other countries? Just click on this map at this site and, before you know it, you'll be surfing through the government Net files of Poland, Israel, Turkey, France, and the like!

### The Prime Minister's Official Residence in Japan HL P

http://www.kantei.go.jp/

Drop in on the Japanese Prime Minister, but don't be disappointed to find he's not at home. As the Web page says, this is "only an experimental service, not an official service." However, you can still check out the "Prime Minister's official residence information" and other Japanese Government Web sites.

### Statistics Canada DF HL

http://WWW.StatCan.CA/
gopher://talon3.statcan.ca/

Get your stats here! Statistics Canada collects numerical information on just about every part of Canada's society and economy. One of things it keeps track of is the population — the number of people who live in Canada. Check it out!

### Thomas: Legislative Information on the Net HL

http://thomas.loc.gov/

What is the U.S. government really up to? Find out here. Take a look at bills going through Congress, especially the hot bills that are being fiercely debated. Discover how the laws are made and look up the e-mail addresses for members of the House of Representatives and the Senate. Go-pher it!

### United Nations HL

gopher://nywork1.undp.org/11/

What exactly is the United Nations (UN) and what does it do? Mole your way into the UN through this Gopher and find out. Check out current UN info, world enviro info, and way more. Get to know the UN!

### United Nations: Voices of Youth  P
http://www.iisd.ca/linkages/un/original.html

The United Nations invites you to speak your mind. Find out what the UN is up to and how you can get involved. Send e-mail to world leaders, check out messages sent to kids by world leaders, and read messages from kids all over the world. Make your voice heard!

### Welcome to the White House  P S
http://www.whitehouse.gov/

Here's your invitation to meet the First Family, take a tour of the White House, send the President and Vice President e-mail, search for government info, check out the President's speeches, and read the White House's press releases. Have a blast!

### White House Information
gopher://gopher.tamu.edu/11/.dir/president.dir

This site brings White House and U.S.-government information right within the reach of your mouse. Discover how to send e-mail to Congress and search the Gopher index for info on domestic issues, international issues, and more.

## HISTORY

### Benjamin Franklin: Glimpses of the Man  HL M P S
http://sln.fi.edu/franklin/rotten.html

Benjamin Franklin is best known for discovering electricity, but electricity is only one of many things he was tinkering with. At this site, you'll get the scoop on Ben's cool inventions, find out about electricity, listen to a thunderbolt, and do lots of other radical stuff. Ben's inventive spirit is alive on the Net!

### The Berlin Wall Falls  M P S
http://192.253.114.31/Berlin/Introduction/Berlin.html

These amazing Web pages have been created by high-school students to mark the fifth anniversary of the fall of the Berlin Wall. After the Second World War, the city of Berlin was split between the Allied Forces — the U.S., Britain, and France — and the former Soviet Union. Eventually, a wall was built between the two halves of the city. But in 1989, the wall was torn down, bringing the city together after 45 years.

### Canadian Museum of Civilization  P
http://www.cmcc.muse.digital.ca/cmc/cmceng/welcmeng.html

Come to the Canadian Museum of Civilization and explore the history of Canada. Go on the Children's Museum's Great Adventure, check out the National Postal Museum, and find out about the behind-the-scenes workings of the museum.

### Canadisk Canadian History Archive  P
http://schoolnet2.carleton.ca/cdisk/english.html

Trying to get the picture? The historical picture, that is? Then you've come to the right place. You'll find over 2000 Canadian historical pictures here. You can browse through the photo collections of people, places, events, and culture to find what you're looking for.

### Flints and Stones  P
http://www.ncl.ac.uk/~nantiq/menu.html

Hang on to your mouse as you blast thousands of years back in time — into the Stone Age! Back then, thick sheets of ice covered large parts of the Earth and mammoths roamed the plains. This site is your ticket to a rockin' adventure!

### Historical Documents
gopher://vax.queens.lib.ny.us/11[gopher._ss._histdocs]

Sometimes you just have to go-pher it — especially when you're looking for historical documents. You'll find an awesome collection here: the Declaration of Independence, Martin Luther King's "I Have a Dream" speech, and Nelson Mandela's inauguration speech, to name just a few.

### Samuel de Champlain
http://info.ic.gc.ca/champlain/history.html

Here's where you can get the scoop on Samuel de Champlain, a.k.a. the "Father of New France." This French Explorer first set foot in Canada in 1603 and later founded the first French settlement in the New World. Park your mouse here to find out more!

### The Viking Network Web  M P
http://odin.nls.no/viking/vnethome.htm

Were the Vikings really known for mortal combat? This Norwegian Web site is the place to go to find out. It will tell you about the Vikings' everyday lives, their travels, and their culture. Vikings rule!

## INSECTS

### Ask Betty the Bug Lady  HL P S
http://www.nj.com/yucky/betty/index.html

When Dr. Betty Faber was a kid, she was completely terrified of flying cockroaches — and completely fascinated by them. Today she's an insect expert, or entomologist, and a bona fide authority on cockroaches. Send her your buggy questions here.

### University of Florida's Book of Insect Records
http://gnv.ifas.ufl.edu/~tjw/recbkprf.htm

The University of Florida's Book of Insect Records is like the Guinness Book of World Records for bugs and creepy crawlies. Click through it and you'll discover the fastest flying insect, the fastest wing-beating insect, the smallest insect eggs, and tons of other buggy stuff.

### GEARS: Global Entomology & Agriculture Research Server  HL P S
http://gears.tucson.ars.ag.gov/

Put your mouse in gear and check out some insect stories, articles, photos, sounds, and facts that will make your skin crawl. Bug off, dude!

### Insect Graphics  HL M P
http://www.life.uiuc.edu/Entomology/graphics.html

Got a bad case of bug love? Come to this Web site and you're sure to find a cure among the tons of cool bug drawings, photos, and movies. Ain't bug love grand?

### Monarch Watch  P
http://129.237.246.134/

Home of the Monarch Watch research project (see p. 19), this site is just jam-packed with info about monarch butterflies. It has answers to frequently asked questions, the story of monarch migration, migration mysteries, monarchs' life stages, a milkweed handbook, and much, much more!

### On the Wings of a Dragonfly  P
http://loki.ur.utk.edu/ut2kids/dragonfly/dragonfly.html

Believe it or not, scientists are trying to design plane wings to flow through the air as efficiently as dragonfly wings. Click your way to the inside story on these fascinating insects in this radical hypertext article.

### UD Entomology Homepage  P
gopher://bluehen.ags.udel.edu:71/hh/.insects/.descriptions/entohome.html

This site is guaranteed to bug you. It's an online insect database! But don't let the scientific names — lepidoptera for butterfly — drive you buggy; when you click on them they're explained. The database gives you info about each insect's body, where it lives, and how it affects our world. Go buggy!

### The Yuckiest Site on the Internet  M P S
http://www.nj.com/yucky/

This site really is the yuckiest site on the Net: it's cockroach central! Check out fun facts, a day in the life of Rodney the cockroach, cockroach Tall Tales, movies and sounds, places roaches call home, Betty the Bug Lady, and more. Yuck out!

◆ ◆ ◆ ◆ ◆ ◆ ◆ ◆ ◆ ◆

## CYBERSTOP

### The Amazing Fish Cam!  HL P
http://www2.netscape.com/fishcam/fishcam.html

Surf with the fish on the Net! This amazing fish cam takes pictures of exotic aquarium fish and sends them to a computer which sends them to the Net. These groovy pics are updated every few minutes. "Netting a fish" has taken on a whole new meaning!

◆ ◆ ◆ ◆ ◆ ◆ ◆ ◆ ◆ ◆

## INTERNATIONAL KIDS PAGES

### The Canadian Kids' Home Page  HL
http://www.onramp.ca/~lowens/107kids.htm

Get ready to surf the ultimate wave. This page is stuffed to the max with awesome hotlinks to cool Net hangouts and sites. Ready, set, catch the wave!

### The Children's Page from Italy  HL
http://www.pd.astro.it/local-cgi-bin/kids.cgi/forms

You are entering a hotlink zone. Prepare to travel to a green world of frogs, play with wooden toys, drop by the BookNook, and take a trip across the universe. Click away!

### The Children's Page  HL P S
http://www.comlab.ox.ac.uk/oucl/users/jonathan.bowen/children.html

Meet Emma and Alice Bowen, sisters who live in the United Kingdom, and check out the cool Web pages they've created. You'll find jokes, stories, poems, and lots of interesting sights and sounds.

### Global Show 'n' Tell  HL
http://emma.manymedia.com:80/show-n-tell/

Hey cybernauts, it's time for show 'n' tell on the Net! Check out other kids' favorite projects, possessions, accomplishments, and collections. And submit your own!

### United Nations: Voices of Youth
http://www.iisd.ca/linkages/un/original.html

The United Nations invites you to speak your mind. Find out what the UN is up to and how you can get involved. Send e-mail to world leaders, check out messages sent to kids by world leaders, and read messages from kids all over the world. Make your voice heard!

## K.O.O.L. — KIDS ONLY ONLINE

### Club Bulletin Board  C PRO
Jump: CLUB BB

Jump onto this bulletin board if you're 12 or under. Post a note or read a note about your favorite (or not-so-favorite) movies, TV shows, books, games, bands, current events . . . the list goes on!

### FreeZone  C HL P
http://freezone.com/

Just call the FreeZone the active zone. Here you can meet cyberpals, play games, giggle, eyeball a flashy e-zine, find out about news that really matters, surf around the world, and way, way more. What are you waiting for?

### Kids  C
joinkids@vms.cis.pitt.edu

Want to talk to other kids over the Net? Then send an e-mail to this address saying you'd like to join and get ready to post away!

### KIDLINK  C
http://www.kidlink.org/

Now here's a cool Net hangout. KIDLINK's a global village where everyone is 10 to 15 years old! Drop by the KIDCAFE to meet new cyberpals and chat a while. Join KIDLINK — it's free — and take part in special projects and discussions.

### KIDLINK Internet Relay Chat  C
http://www.kidlink.org/IRC/

Get set to chat to other kids on the Net in real time. Hop on the KIDLINK IRC channel, find out what's happening, and before you know it you'll be chattering, er, typing away!

### Kids' Corner  HL
http://www.ot.com:80/cgi/public/imagemap/ht/kids/map.kids?60,238

Hey cybersurfer, grab your surfboard and surf these radical hotlinks all around the Net. Visit science, reading, sports, games, and "just for fun" sites. Go art-museum hopping, too.

### Kids on Campus  HL
http://www.tc.cornell.edu/Kids.on.Campus/WWWDemo/

Kids are everywhere! Here's a cool collection of hotlinks that will send you surfing all over the Net. Enjoy the sights and sounds.

### KidsCom: A Communication Playground  C HL P S
http://www.kidscom.com/

Have fun surfing in this cyberplayground where you can find a cyberpal, write some graffiti, post pictures and stories about your pet, write stories, play games, and do lots of other cool stuff.

### Kids' Crossing: The Voice of Rocky Mountain Youth  C HL
http://rmii.com/~pachecod/kidsnet/kidscross.html

Just surfing through? Stop by the Colorado Kids' Crossing to meet cyberpals, chat on bulletin boards, play games, hotlink to great Internet adventures, learn how to write HTML, and more!

### Radio Aahs Online  M P S
http://www.radio-aahs.com

Radio Aahs, the kids' 24-hour radio network, blasts the cyberwaves! This site is packed with lots of cool stuff: late-breaking news, puzzles and fun, kids' heroes, top-10 lists, interviews with stars, and reviews of books, movies, CDs, and video games. There's even a place where you can ask for advice about tough problems or questions — aaaahht last!

### Scholastic's Kids World  C AOL
Go to Kids Only

Zip into Kids World and have some cool chats with some cool cats. Hang out at these message boards and you can meet kids from all over the world and talk about whatever's on your mind.

◆ ◆ ◆ ◆ ◆ ◆ ◆ ◆ ◆ ◆ ◆

## CYBERSTOP

### The World Right Now  P
http://www.cam-orl.co.uk/world.html

Here's a virtual window on the world at large. This site is linked to lots of live outdoor cameras around the world. Just click on the world map and take a look at what's happening in Germany, England, Sweden, Scotland, Norway, or other countries. Snap to it!

◆ ◆ ◆ ◆ ◆ ◆ ◆ ◆ ◆ ◆ ◆

## MATH

### Ask Dr. Math
http://forum.swarthmore.edu/dr.math/dr-math.html

Stumped by a mind-boggling math question? Search Dr. Math's archives for expertly explained solutions to similar problems. And if all else fails, e-mail it to the Swat Team at Ask Dr. Math. They'll deboggle it and send you a step-by-step solution. Swat that!

### Blue Dog Can Count  S
http://fedida.ini.cmu.edu:5550/bdf.html

This little dog's got a lot to woof about. She can count, add, multiply, and divide. Go, Blue Dog, Go!

### The Geometry Center Picture Archive
http://www.geom.umn.edu/pix/archive/top.html

The pics at this site are coo-oo-ool. They're like candy for the eyes! But the really radical thing about them is that they've been created with math. Now who says math isn't cool?

### Math Magic
http://www.scri.fsu.edu/~dennisl/topics/math_magic.html

And now for a little math magic. You don't have to be a math wiz to do these amazing magic tricks. Try them out on your friends and see if they catch on to the math that makes the tricks work.

## MOVIES

### Walt Disney  M P S
http://www.disney.com/

Here's where you can find out about current and upcoming movies, television, and music from Walt Disney. Try out an interactive movie adventure or take a sneak peek at some movie clips and interviews with the director, producer, actors, and crew. Roll 'em!

### Hollywood Online  M P S
http://www.hollywood.com:80/

Pack your mouse and head for Hollywood! At this Web site, you can check out movies that are currently playing, watch trailers, look at photos, read movie notes, and more.

### The Internet Movie Database  HL P
http://www.cm.cf.ac.uk/Movies/

This movie database is loaded with lots of cool information on just about any movie you can name. Park your mouse here and click through the crazy credits, movie goofs, ratings, production information, and photos.

### MovieWeb  DF HL M P
http://movieweb.com/movie/movie.html

This is your ticket to the movies on the Net. Download movie previews, posters, photos, and notes. Check out last weekend's top 25 movies at the box office, and then surf the hotlinks to movie Web pages.

### Silicon Studio  M P

http://www.studio.sgi.com/

Step into the Silicon Studio and take a peek at some of the hottest special effects around. Walk down the Avenue of Stars to see some cool special effects and then click on "Interactive Entertainment" to find out about virtual reality.

### Space Movie Archive  DF M P S

http://www.univ-rennes1.fr/ASTRO/anim-e.html

Hey, space movie buffs! Park your mouse here and get set to download solar eclipses, sci-fi faves (including Star Trek), the Jupiter comet crash, space missions, lunar probes, and lots of other goodies.

### The Star Wars Home Page  DF HL M P S

http://stwing.resnet.upenn.edu:8001/
~jruspini/starwars.html

Surf back in time to a galaxy far, far away . . . and enter the Star Wars zone. This site has got Star Wars movie clips, sound files, trivia, games, news, and much, much more. May the Force be with you!

## CYBERSTOP

### Hot Lava Lamp  M

http://ascott.com/hal/htmls/lava.html

Hang with some cool morphin' cats and watch chunks of lava flow by at Hal's funky lava lamp. Hot stuff!

## MUSEUMS

### Canadian Museum of Civilization  P

http://www.cmcc.muse.digital.ca/cmc/cmceng/
welcmeng.html

Come to the Canadian Museum of Civilization and explore the history of Canada. Go on the Children's Museum's Great Adventure, check out the National Postal Museum, and find out about the behind-the-scenes workings of the museum.

### The Computer Museum

http://www.net.org/

Enter the Computer Museum's online Internet Sampler and you'll get the lowdown on the inner workings of the Net and the Net's effect on our world. Then check out what the kids at the Computer Clubhouse are up to and take a tour of their online art gallery.

### Exploratorium Home Page  HL M P S

http://www.exploratorium.edu/

Get set to virtually explore the Exploratorium. This site has got some of the coolest online exhibits on the Net: mutant fruit flies, vocal vowels, and a fading dot, to name just a few. Drop by the Learning Studio to check out all this and more. Walk right in!

### The Field Museum of Natural History  M P S

http://www.bvis.uic.edu/museum/Dna_To_
Dinosaurs.html

Start your tour by clicking on "Exhibits" and get set to explore life over time — from DNA to dinosaurs. Test out the multimedia goodies to see Triceratops run and Moropus eat, play an interactive game to test your knowledge of camel anatomy, and then listen to some mammoth-bone music. Have a blast!

### The Franklin Institute Science Museum  HL M P S

http://sln.fi.edu/

Rev up your mouse and take a virtual tour of the Franklin Institute. Catch some glimpses of Benjamin Franklin and his electric discoveries, and then virtually explore the human heart. Surf to the beat!

### Musée du Louvre  HL P

http://meteora.ucsd.edu/~norman/paris/
Musees/Louvre/

Touch down in Paris, France, and check out the Mona Lisa's smile at the Louvre. The Louvre holds many of the world's priceless treasures. Take a look at its collections of Egyptian, Oriental, Roman, and Greek objets d'art. Then click your way around "gay Paree"!

### Smithsonian Institution: National Museum of Natural History  HL P

http://nmnhwww.si.edu/nmnhweb.html

Believe it or not, the Smithsonian Institution has over 120 million cultural artifacts and science specimens in its collections. Of course, you won't find them all here. But you can still wind your way through this natural history Web to find pictures and information about them. Don't be put off if you have to do a little Gophering!

### Treasures of the Czars  P S

http://www.times.st-pete.fl.us/
Treasures/Default.html

Check out the treasures of the Russian czars by clicking on "Museum Tour." Then drop by the "Playground of the Czars" to take a crash course in Russian, scroll through amazing Russian facts, find out about Russian books, and lots more. Rush on over!

### University of California Museum of Paleontology  P

http://ucmp1.berkeley.edu/exhibittext/entrance.
html

Step into the museum's geological time machine and ride millions of years back in time to see what the Earth was like way back when. Or take the Web lift to any group of animals from fleas to sharks to dinosaurs. Virtually exploring the California Museum of Paleontology is a real blast!

## MUSIC

### FTP Music Archives  P

ftp://mirrors.aol.com:/pub/music/

This is the place to go to for info about your favorite bands. Here you'll find cool band photos, song lyrics, guitar chords for your favorite songs, info about new CD releases, and more.

### The History of Rock 'n' Roll  HL M P S

http://www.hollywood.com:80/rocknroll/

Get the lowdown on the history of rock from legends such as Bono, Madonna, David Bowie, Eddie Van Halen, Bruce Springsteen, Pete Townshend, Alice Cooper, Tina Turner, and Steven Tyler. And take a peek at some legendary pics and videos.

### MTV  M P S

http://www.mtv.com/

Get your MTV fix on the Net! Here's where you can check out music news bites, new releases, and MTV's sights and sounds. Rock on!

### MuchMusic  M P

http://www.muchmusic.com/muchmusic.html

How much is too much? Well . . . you can never have too much music. At this site, you can watch cool video clips of your favorite bands, request a video, and check the MuchMusic top-30 count-down.  And if you've really got something on your mind, hop into the electronic Speaker's Corner and unload it.

### OLGA: Online Guitar Archive

ftp://ftp.nevada.edu/pub/guitar/

Got a guitar? Enjoy singing, strumming, rocking, and rapping to your favorite songs? Then this is definitely the place to go. Check out the song lyrics and guitar chords to lots of groovy tunes. Start jamming!

### The Rolling Stones Web Site  DF HL M P S

http://www.stones.com/

Drop by the Voodoo Lounge to hang out with the Stones. Surf through the ultimate band site: listen to the Stones live, watch them on video, read interviews with them, and check out cool Stones' pics. Send in your "burning" questions and they'll try to answer them. The Stones roll on!

### Top Hits Online  HL

http://www.softdisk.com/comp/hits/

This is a weekly music chart that you and your fellow cybersurfers around the world control. Vote for your top 15 songs each week and then check out the results.

### The Ultimate Band List  HL P S

http://american.recordings.com/wwwofmusic/
ubl/ubl.shtml

Here's a virtual band city that really rocks — prepare to ride the ultimate wave! The Ultimate Band List has the ultimate hotlinks to bands, bands, and more bands on the Net. Find out about cool band news, World Wide Web pages, lyrics, and way more.

## CYBERSTOP

### Interactive Model Railroad  HL M P

http://www-vs.informatik.uni-ulm.de/RR/
RR.html

Hitch a ride on the interactive express in Germany. Choose an engine and a destination and watch the train go. All aboard!

# SCHOOLS ON THE NET

## The CyberSpace Middle School  HL P
http://www.scri.fsu.edu/~dennisl/CMS.html

The CyberSpace Middle School is "not just a school, but an adventure." Drop by and ride a virtual school bus around the Net, read about the school's special projects, and surf their hotlinks to cool places on the Web. Surf's up, dude!

## Global Schoolhouse
http://k12.cnidr.org/gsh/gshwelcome.html

The Global Schoolhouse was started to link kids around the world to the Net to explore the high-tech world of information technology. This site lists the projects that the kids did and the schools that participated. Check it out!

## Hillside Elementary School  M P
http://hillside.coled.umn.edu/

This Web site has been created by the kids at Hillside Elementary School in Minnesota. And they've packed it with lots of radical stuff. Read the Buzz Rod story and choose your own ending (from 22 possible endings in all!). Check out the kids' projects and book reviews, too.

## Patch American High School
http://192.253.114.31/Home.html

This American high school in Stuttgart, Germany, has wired all kinds of exciting stuff into their Web site. Check out their Berlin Wall Falls project, video productions, Internet class, poetry, stereograms, and virtual field trips. Patch in!

## SchoolNet
http://schoolnet2.carleton.ca/

Want to find out what schools are hooked up to the Net? Check out SchoolNet's White Pages. It lists schools in Canada and around the world. The SchoolNet Resource Manual is another great reference, too. It lists the top 100 science and technology resources on the Internet. SchoolNet keeps your mouse on the pulse!

## Web 66: A K12 World Wide Web  HL
http://web66.coled.umn.edu/

Speed down Web 66 and check out the schools that are on the Net. Web 66 keeps the "Internet's oldest and most far-reaching list of kindergarten to grade 12 servers" around the world.

# SCIENCE

## Amethyst Galleries' Mineral Gallery  P
http://mineral.galleries.com/

This site is a rock hound's dream. It's packed with great pics of rocks and minerals, and it has an electronic index of interesting information about minerals such as diamonds, emeralds, and rubies. Rock on!

## The Art of Renaissance Science  HL P S
http://bang.lanl.gov/video/stv/arshtml/arstoc.html

Travel back in time about 400 years to the age of the Renaissance and find out about the "art of science." This site focuses on the radical experiments of the Italian mathematician Galileo and the importance of mathematics to Renaissance art.

## Benjamin Franklin: Glimpses of the Man  HL M P S
http://sln.fi.edu/franklin/rotten.html

Benjamin Franklin is best known for discovering electricity, but electricity is only one of many things he was tinkering with. At this site, you'll get the scoop on Ben's cool inventions, find out about electricity, listen to a thunderbolt, and do lots of other radical stuff. Ben's inventive spirit is alive on the Net!

## Dante II  HL M P
http://maas-neotek.arc.nasa.gov/Dante/dante.html

Meet a robot that has gone where no man has gone before — into the fiery depths of a volcano! Scientists controlled this walking robot as it plunged into Alaska's Mt. Spurr volcano to collect gas samples. Look at photos of Dante in action and the photos it took on this amazing mission.

## The Future Is Yours  HL P
http://loki.ur.utk.edu/ut2kids/scientists/girlsintro.html

What do you want to be when you grow up? When Dr. Arlene Garrison was in grade three, the first rockets were blasting into space, and that's when she decided she wanted to be a scientist. Today she's a chemist. Meet her along with a geologist and a physicist and find out about their awesome jobs.

## The Heart: A Virtual Exploration  M P S
http://sln.fi.edu/biosci/heart.html

Did you know that your heart is the same size as your fist? That's just one of the neat things you'll discover as you virtually explore the human heart at this site. Listen to a heart beat, follow blood through blood vessels, watch a surgeon perform open-heart surgery, and find out how to take your pulse. Click to the beat!

## The Jason Project  C DF HL P S
http://seawifs.gsfc.nasa.gov/scripts/JASON.html

Surf into this site and explore the mysteries of the deep blue sea with JASON, a research robot that dives into the deep. Every year, the JASON Project explores a different fascinating part of the world and broadcasts each expedition as it happens. That way, kids all over the world can see what scientists are doing and discovering. This site is packed with project info, expedition journals, and discussion groups. Dive in!

## Matt's Solar Car Page  HL P
http://www-lips.ece.utexas.edu/~delayman/solar.html

Zoom into this solar zone where you'll find cool pictures and information about solar cars. You can get the inside track on solar car racing, too. Solar rules!

## Mercury Project: Robotic Tele-Excavation  HL M P
http://cwis.usc.edu:80/dept/raiders/

The Net is a powerful tool. Think about this: it allowed millions of people to take part in an archaeological dig without ever leaving home. How? They used the Net to send commands to a robot that was working at a simulated dig. Sound crazy? Find out about this cool project here and surf the hotlinks to find similar projects that are happening around the Net now.

## Monarch Watch  P
http://129.237.246.134/

Home of the Monarch Watch research project (see p. 19), this site is just jam-packed with info about monarch butterfies. It has answers to frequently asked questions, the story of monarch migration, migration mysteries, monarchs' life stages, a milkweed handbook, and much, much more!

## NetFrog: Interactive Frog Dissection  M P
http://curry.edschool.Virginia.EDU:80/~insttech/frog/

Hold your mouse steady, get set, and . . . cut. Using your mouse to virtually dissect a frog is one of the most radical things you can do on the Web! This site takes you through a frog dissection step-by-step. Learn to identify the organs inside a frog's body such as the heart, liver, and kidneys. Cool stuff!

## Nye Labs  HL M P S
http://www.seanet.com/Vendors/billnye/nyelabs.html

Bill Nye the Science Guy is kicking up a blast in cyberspace. Check out this way cool u-NYE-verse where science rules the waves. It's hotlinked to oodles of great science sites!

## Ontario Science Centre  HL P
http://www.osc.on.ca/

Cruise into the Ontario Science Centre where science is always hip and happenin'. Check the weather forecast, thumb through an Internet newspaper that links you to cool stuff going on around the world, and check out the center's awesome hotlinks.

## Science Bytes  HL P
http://loki.ur.utk.edu/ut2Kids/science.html

Science has got real bite. Just check out these Science Byte articles that talk about the work being done by scientists at the University of Tennessee. You'll meet a scientist who's mad about marmosets, find out how maps are made, and discover other radical stuff. If there's something you really want to know about, ask them by e-mail

### Search for Antarctic Spring HL P
http://loki.ur.utk.edu/ut2kids/penguins/penguin.html

Join 20 scientists as they sail through the cold Antarctic waters in search of phytoplankton, tiny sea plants which bloom in the early spring. These microscopic plants provide food for lots of sea animals. Click on the hypertext in this article to see photos and find out more. Surf and read!

### TOPEX/Poseidon Online DF HL P
http://quest.arc.nasa.gov/topex/welcome.html

TOPEX/Poseidon's mission is to develop and operate a satellite system that observes the ocean. You'll find lots of neat stuff here: images from the satellite, day-in-the-life journals of the people who run the satellite, questions and answers, and more.

### The Virtual Hospital P
http://indy.radiology.uiowa.edu/Welcome/UIHC/museum/web.CompMus/CompMus/01Introduction.html

The Net could be good for your health. To find out more, do the demo of the Virtual Hospital at this site. One day you may use the Net to find medical information that could save your life. Check it out!

### VolcanoWorld P
http://volcano.und.nodak.edu/

Ooh! Aah! This site is hot, hot, hot! VolcanoWorld sizzles with news and current events about volcanoes, information about how to become a volcanologist, photos of recent eruptions and volcanoes around the world, and more.

### A World in Motion M
http://schoolnet2.carleton.ca/cgi-bin/search/mfs/01/math_sci/phys/worldinmotion/index.html

If you like to get moving, power up, slow down, move easy, and get airborne all in the name of science, then this site is for you. It's got lots of step-by-step experiments and activities that you can do to investigate the world in motion.

## SPACE

### The Apollo Mission to the Moon HL M P S
http://www.gsfc.nasa.gov/hqpao/apollo_11.html

Beam your mouse to the moon! This is the place to find out all about the historic space mission that put man on the moon. Check out movies, photos, sound files, and the astronauts' memories of the mission. Get moonwalking!

### Bradford Robotic Telescope DF HL P
http://www.telescope.org/rti/

Want to have a telescope take a picture of the night sky? This site feeds "jobs" to a robotic telescope that's located in England. You say where you want the telescope to look, then the job is sent to the telescope, and the results come back in a couple of days. You even get to download images from your job. Try it!

### Canada's Astronauts P
http://schoolnet2.carleton.ca/cgi-bin/search/mfs/01/math_sci/astronauts/index.html

Meet Canada's astronauts and find out about their interests, training, secrets of success, and how they prepare for missions. Check out the Canadian Space Station Program, too!

### Canadian Space Agency HL P
http://www.dsm.sp-agency.ca/

Blast your way into space with the Canadian Space Agency and find out about the Canadian Astronaut Program, space science and technology, the international space station, and lots of other racy spacy stuff.

### The Canadian Space Guide HL P
http://www.conveyor.com/space.html

Bring your mouse in for a landing here and check out the latest news flashes from the Canadian space program. Find out about the program's projects and check out the calendar of Canadian space events, too. Blast on in!

### Comet Shoemaker-Levy Home Page DF HL M P
http://newproducts.jpl.nasa.gov:80/sl9/sl9.html

Look out — head-on collision straight ahead! Take a look at the spectacular crash of Comet Shoemaker-Levy into Jupiter. You'll find lots of cool photos and amazing animations here, along with information and newsflashes galore.

### Jet Propulsion Laboratory Image/Information Archives HL P
http://www.jpl.nasa.gov/archive/

This is the place where you can get your hands on awesome space pics, fact sheets, and news about the Jet Propulsion Laboratory's space missions. Happy hunting!

### Liftoff to Space Exploration DF HL M P
http://liftoff.msfc.nasa.gov/

Gear up to blast into space at this site. Attend the Lift Off Academy and learn about the shuttle, microgravity, and what it takes to be an astronaut or a rocket scientist. Check past, present, and future missions, and liftoff into space on a virtual reality trip!

### NASA Space Link HL
http://spacelink.msfc.nasa.gov/

Link up to Space Link and find out what's happening at NASA. Check out hot topics, NASA news, NASA projects, questions and answers, and educational services. NASA rocks the Net!

### The Nine Planets: A Multimedia Tour of the Solar System HL M P S
http://seds.lpl.arizona.edu/nineplanets/nineplanets/nineplanets.html

Get set to go planet hopping! On this way-cool multimedia tour of our solar system's nine planets, you can also visit the sun and the moon. Find out neat planet facts, and check out some awesome planet pics and movies. Blast off!

### Project Galileo: Bringing Jupiter to Earth HL P
http://www.jpl.nasa.gov:80/galileo/

Galileo, an unmanned spacecraft, travelled millions of kilometers (miles) into space to launch a probe toward Jupiter. The probe's mission: to study the planet's atmosphere and its moons. Touch down at this site to find out how Galileo "phones home" and to get the inside story on the project!

### SETI: Search for Extraterrestrial Intelligence
http://www.seti-inst.edu/

Are any extra-terrestrial beings really out there? It's SETI's job to find out. SETI says "there are billions of places outside our solar system that may contain life." But so far none has been discovered. Park your mouse here to find out more.

### Spacelink Hot Topics M P
http://spacelink.msfc.nasa.gov:80/Spacelink.Hot.Topics/

Here's a handy shortcut that will take you straight to the really hot topics at NASA. It's updated often, so check it regularly to find out what's cooking!

### Space Movie Archive DF M
http://www.univ-rennes1.fr/ASTRO/anim-e.html

Hey, space movie buffs! Park your mouse here and get set to download: solar eclipses, sci-fi faves (including Star Trek), the Jupiter comet crash, space missions, lunar probes, and lots of other goodies.

### The StarChild Project: Connecting NASA and the K12 Classroom HL M P S
http://guinan.gsfc.nasa.gov/K12/StarChild.html

How far away are the stars? What is a galaxy? Bone up on your astronomy basics at this site. And check out a radical animation of the Big Bang that created the universe!

### Views of the Solar System M P
http://www.c3.lanl.gov/~cjhamil/SolarSystem/homepage.html

Take this awesome virtual tour of the solar system that's loaded with photos and animations of the planets, interesting information about space missions, and facts about comets, meteorites and much, much more. This site is guaranteed to take you out of this world!

### Welcome to the Planets P
http://stardust.jpl.nasa.gov/planets/

As you flyby the planets on this virtual tour, you'll get a chance to see each one up close (as close as we can get for now)! Take a good look at the canyons on Mars, the Great Red Spot on Jupiter, the rings around Saturn, and other interesting features that mark the alien worlds in our own solar system's back yard.

# SPORTS

## The Age of Sail DF HL
http://www.cs.yale.edu/homes/sjl/sail.html

Sail to this site to find lots of sailing clip art and hotlinks to sailing sites anchored around the Net. Bon voyage!

## Major League Baseball P
http://www2.pcy.mci.net:80/mlb/index.html

Step up to the plate and check out the latest baseball scores and stats, news and notes, and awesome shots of players. Batter up!

## DansWorld Skateboarding HL M P
http://www.cps.msu.edu/~dunhamda/dw/dansworld.html

Skate into DansWorld and check out some cool photos of big airs, noseslides, and stalefishes, watch some skateboarding movies, and surf the hotlinks to other skateboarding sites around the Net.

## Figure Skating Home Page HL M P
http://www.cs.yale.edu/HTML/YALE/CS/HyPlans/loosemore-sandra/skate.html

Park your mouse here and before you know it, it'll be doing double axels and triple flip jumps. You'll find great shots of skaters, neat technical info (How did those jumps get such weird names?), cool videos of the jumps and spins, and lots more. Glide on in!

## Jason's Web Kite Site HL P
http://www.latrobe.edu.au/Glenn/KiteSite/Kites.html

Kool kites rule the skies. Chinese dragons, tumbling cubes, and rainbow birds are just a few of the kites that fly high in Jason's photos. But if you want to see something really radical, check out the kite buggy pics. A kite buggy is like a go-kart attached to a kite. These curious contraptions can zoom along the Australian outback at speeds up to 80 km/h (50 mph)!

## Matt's Solar Car Page HL P
http://www-lips.ece.utexas.edu/~delayman/solar.html

Zoom into this solar zone where you'll find cool pictures and information about solar cars. You can get the inside track on solar car racing, too. Solar rules!

## The Michael Jordan Page HL P
http://gagme.wwa.com/~boba/mj1.html

Enter the Michael Jordan zone. Here you'll find great pics, info about the great one's career, career stats, and lots of links to other Jordan info on the Net. Zone out!

## NHL Open Net P S
http://www.nhl.com/

Grab your hockey stick, er, mouse and skate around the official NHL arena on the Web. This is the place where you can find out about the latest hockey news, events, scores and stats, teams, history, rules, and more!

## Reebok Athlete Interviews
http://www.planetreebok.com/interview.html

Chat with a great athlete online! Dates and times for athlete interviews are posted here, so surf by often to find out what's happening.

## The Snow Page HL P
http://rmd-www.mr.ic.ac.uk/snow/snowpage.html

Get set to ski into the flakiest site on Web — The Snow Page! Here you'll find info about skiing, snowboarding, and lots of cool links. Brrrrr!

## Sports GIFs DF P
ftp://nic.funet.fi/pub/sports/PICTURES/gif/

Looking for some great pics of your favorite athletes? Park your mouse here and download away! This site has some great basketball, hockey, figure skating, biking, football, skiing, rock climbing, and windsurfing shots. Check out the rockin' rollercoaster shots, too!

## Sports Illustrated for Kids Online P
http://www.pathfinder.com/@@WqCNLgAAAAAAADAK/SIFK/index.html

Sports Illustrated for Kids Online is loaded with lots of neat stuff. Check out the articles and facts on world-class athletes, athletes that share your birthday, kids' art and stories, sports tips, and the SI for Kids Challenge. Surf on in, dude!

## World Wide Web of Sports HL M P
http://www.tns.lcs.mit.edu/cgi-bin/sports

The Netspiders who spun this Web weren't kidding when they called it the World Wide Web of Sports. This Web covers basketball, football, the Olympics, horse racing, sailing, hockey, baseball, soccer, golf, car racing, frisbee, gymnastics, volleyball, cycling, windsurfing, rugby, running, skating, cricket, tennis, wrestling, surfing, skateboarding, and more. Sports rule!

◆ ◆ ◆ ◆ ◆ ◆ ◆ ◆ ◆ ◆

# CYBERSTOP

## Fallscam DF HL M P
http://fallscam.niagara.com/

This site has made a real splash on the Net. It's got pictures and videos of Niagara Falls in action. Bring your towel!

◆ ◆ ◆ ◆ ◆ ◆ ◆ ◆ ◆ ◆

# The Tube — TV

## The Discovery Channel Canada HL
http://www.discovery.ca/default.htm

Find out what there is to discover at the Discovery Channel. Check out their weekly program listings, tell them what you think about their shows, and follow their hotlinks to interesting sites on the Net. It's yours to discover!

## Goosebumps™
http://www.scholastic.com/public/Goosebumps/Cover.html

If you're a fan of R.L. Stine's scary Goosebumps books, touch down here and find out about the TV show based on the books. Check out upcoming episodes and an interview with the scaremeister author himself. Don't get spooked!

## The History of Rock 'n' Roll HL M P S
http://www.hollywood.com:80/rocknroll/

Get the lowdown on the history of rock from legends such as Bono, Madonna, David Bowie, Eddie Van Halen, Bruce Springsteen, Pete Townshend, Alice Cooper, Tina Turner, and Steven Tyler. And take a peek at some legendary pics and videos.

## MTV M P S
http://www.mtv.com/

Get your MTV fix on the Net! Here's where you can check out music news bites, new releases, and MTV's sights and sounds. Rock on!

## MuchMusic M P
http://www.muchmusic.com/muchmusic.html

How much is too much? Well . . . you can never have too much music. At this site, you can watch cool video clips of your favorite bands, request a video, and check the MuchMusic top-30 countdown. And if you've really got something on your mind, hop into the electronic Speaker's Corner and unload it.

## Muppets Home Page HL P
http://www.ncsa.uiuc.edu/VR/BS/Muppets/muppets.html

Check out the cyberspace digs of Kermit the Frog, Miss Piggy, and the rest of the Muppet gang. Here you can find out when the Muppets are on TV, cool Muppet info, and much, much more. Surf the hotlinks to fab Muppet pics and songs!

## Nickelodeon P
http://www.ee.surrey.ac.uk/Contrib/Entertainment/nickelodeon.html

You won't need to put a nickel in this virtual jukebox to find out all about your favorite Nickelodeon shows. Just click on the hypertext and go! Check out the shows' casts, episode guides, interviews with stars, show trivia, and way more!

## Nye Labs HL M P S
http://www.seanet.com/Vendors/billnye/nyelabs.html

Bill Nye the Science Guy is kicking up a blast in cyberspace. Check out this way cool u-NYE-verse where science rules the waves. It's hotlinked to oodles of great science sites!

## The Power Rangers Homepage HL M P S
http://kilp.media.mit.edu:8001/power/homepage.html

This is where the Mighty Morphin' Power Rangers hang on the Net. Get the lowdown on your favorite characters and the actors that play them. Click your way through the monster gallery, picture database, movie clips, sound bites, and lots more!

## The Simpsons DF HL M P S
http://yarrow.wt.com.au/~sjackson/simpsons/

The Simpsons have got lots of addresses in cyberspace. This site will hotlink you to the coolest Simpsons sites, sounds, video clips, and info on the Net. Cowabunga, dude!

### Star Trek Source  HL P S
http://www.cdsnet.net/vidiot/

Trekkin' the Net for Star Trek info? Start here. This site has got Federation Starfleet news, Trek photos, sound bites, TV info, actors' bios, program guides, and a lot more. Happy trekkin'!

### Street Cents Online  P S
http://www.screen.com/streetcents.html

"Street Cents Online is about your money — how to get it and how not to get ripped off when you spend it." The TV show's "young correspondents from across Canada are always looking for what's a deal — and what's not. This is where you can see what they've found out."

### ReBoot!!  DF M P S
http://alliance.idirect.com/reboot/

Proceed with caution: you are now entering the world of Mainframe. Ready, set, ReBoot! Take a tour around Mainframe in your favorite vehicle from the show, and check out your favorite places and characters. Jack in!

### Ultimate TV List  HL
http://tvnet.com/UTVL/utvl.html

Want to find out about your favorite TV show? Then touch down here and start clicking. You'll find episode guides, newsgroups, frequently asked questions, hotlinks to pics, sounds, clips, and way more!

### Warner Brothers' Animation  DF M P S
http://pathfinder.com/@@kTNNdNHf0QEAQGBW/KidsWB/home.html

Get set to meet your favorite cartoon characters from shows such as the Animaniacs, Freakazoid!, Pinky and the Brain, Earthworm Jim, and the Sylvester and Tweety Mysteries. Check out the cool games you can download, too.

◆ ◆ ◆ ◆ ◆ ◆ ◆ ◆ ◆ ◆ ◆

## CYBERSTOP

### Nessie on the Net in Scotland!  HL P
http://www.scotnet.co.uk:80/highland/index.html

Does Nessie rule the loch? Well, we don't know if the Loch Ness monster actually exists. That's all the more reason to click on NessieFax at this site in the Scottish Highlands. Check out "the place Nessie calls home," too.

## VIRTUAL REFERENCES

### Berit's Best Sites for Children  HL
http://www.cochran.com/theosite/Ksites_part1.html#family

Surf the awesome links on Berit's hotlist and you'll catch wave after wave of kids' home pages, science, history, geography, travel, online stories . . . rev up your engines, cybernauts!

### Biographical Dictionary
http://www.mit.edu:8001/afs/athena/activity/c/collegebowl/biog_dict/intro.html

Who is Michelangelo? Nefertiti? Macauley Culkin? Plug in the name of any person who lived from ancient times to the present and this online Biographical Dictionary will give you the basic facts on him or her. Plug away!

### Children's Literature Web Guide  HL
http://www.ucalgary.ca/~dkbrown/index.html

Here's an awesome guide to kid lit — literature, that is — on the Net. Use it to find online stories and books, kids' writing, and online markets for your own writing. Get clicking!

### CRAYON — CreAte Your Own Newspaper  HL
http://sun.bucknell.edu/~boulter/crayon/

Color your world with CRAYON by CreAting Your Own Newspaper! Pick and choose the kinds of news, comic strips, and the like that you want to read everyday and put together your own personal newspaper. It'll be updated daily — CRAYON keeps you current!

### Current Weather Maps/Movies  M P
http://rs560.cl.msu.edu/weather/

Everybody's always talking about the weather. Drop by this site to get the latest info — the weather maps here are updated every hour! And you can click on the Interactive Weather Browser to find out what weather conditions are like in any major North American city!

### Kids Web: A World Wide Web Digital Library for Schoolkids  HL P
http://www.npac.syr.edu:80/textbook/kidsweb/

Take a trip to this virtual library and let your mouse go surfing. This library has got lots of great art, science, math, geography, space, and sports links to explore. And best of all, after you've got the info you need, you won't have to worry about having any overdue books!

### National SchoolNet Atlas
http://www-nais.ccm.emr.ca/schoolnet/

The National SchoolNet Atlas has maps of Canada and the world, facts about Canada, hot topics and issues, and a geographical name search engine. You can also use it to test your knowledge of Canadian geography and to create your own maps. Map a bookmark here!

### Roget's Thesaurus
gopher://odie.niaid.nih.gov:77/.thesaurus/index

When the word you're looking for gets stuck on the tip of your tongue, just plug a synonym into Roget's online thesaurus. Roget's interface may not look like much, but it sure is powerful. Try it and see!

### SchoolNet Gopher  C
gopher://schoolnet.carleton.ca:419/

SchoolNet links Canadian schools to the Internet. Drop by the Virtual School and click on "Recess." Here you'll find KIDLINK and SchoolNet chat newsgroups as well as MUDs, MOOs, and MUSES — virtual realities that are yours to play in. Go-pher it, dude!

### Smithsonian Photos  P
ftp://sunsite.unc.edu/pub/multimedia/pictures/smithsonian/

Looking for a photo of the Hope Diamond, the Apollo spacecraft, Egyptian mummies, elephants, or dino bones? Then look no further! The Smithsonian has a fantastic collection of photos that spans a wide range of topics: air and space, art, people and places, science and nature, and history of technology. Surf and download!

### The Subway  HL
http://ucmp1.berkeley.edu/subway.html

Ride the Subway to lots of cool places on the Net. Just click on the place on the map where you want to go and then sit back and relax. You can get off at the Tree of Life, the Palaeontological Institute of Russia, Expo . . . and then climb aboard for another ride!

### Uncle Bob's Kids' Page  HL
http://gagme.wwa.com:80/~boba/kids.html

Hotlinks galore! This page has got the hottest kid links on the Web. Surf your way through science, sports, games, nature, museums, math, geography, art, TV, movies, and much, much more. Surf's up, dude!

### Weather Information Superhighway  HL M P
http://thunder.met.fsu.edu/nws/public_html/wxhwy.html

This site has everything you ever wanted to know about weather but didn't know who to ask: weather around the world, satellite images, weather radar, climate info, weather maps, weather movies, Gopher servers, Web sites, and — of course — the forecast.

### Webster's Dictionary
http://c.gp.cs.cmu.edu:5103/prog/webster

Plug a word into Webster's online dictionary and let its computer look it up for you. Don't worry if you spell the word incorrectly, the computer will prompt you with correct spelling as it searches — phew! But what makes this dictionary really awesome is that you can look up the words in the definitions with just a click of your mouse.

### The Whole Internet Catalog  HL
http://gnn.digital.com/gnn/wic/index.html

The Whole Internet Catalog is like a Yellow Pages directory for the Net. Let your mouse scroll through the pages until you find the ultimate clickable destination. The Catalog's got more than 1000 links to sites on the Net!

### The WWW Virtual Library  HL

http://www.w3.org/hypertext/DataSources/
bySubject/Overview.html

Whatever topic you're researching, you're bound
to find something on it at the WWW Virtual
Library. And you can click your way through this
library without ever leaving home. When was
research so much fun?

## CYBERSTOP

### IguanaCam  HL  P

http://iguana.images.com/dupecam.html

What's a day in the life of an iguana like? This is
where you can find out. Every couple of minutes
a picture of Dupree the green iguana is taken and
sent to this Web site.

## VISUAL ARTS

### Ansel Adams  P  S

http://bookweb.cwis.uci.edu:8042/Sliced
Exhibit.html

Ansel Adams' black-and-white photographs cap-
ture breathtaking images of the natural world.
You can look at some of his photos in this virtual
exhibit and listen to him talk about them.

### The Art of Renaissance Science  HL  P  S

http://bang.lanl.gov/video/stv/arshtml/arstoc.
html

Travel back in time about 400 years to the age of
the Renaissance and find out about the "art of
science." This site focuses on the radical experiments of the Italian mathematician Galileo and
the importance of mathematics to Renaissance
art.

### Cave Paintings in France  P

http://www.culture.fr/culture/gvpda-en.htm

Cave paintings 17,000 to 20,000 years old were
discovered recently in Vallon, France, when
archaeologists found an unexplored system of
caves. Many of the paintings show animals such
as bears, horses, rhinoceros, wild oxen, and
mammoths. Check 'em out here!

### KidArt Computer Art Gallery

gopher://kids.ccit.duq.edu:70/11/kidart

Here's a gallery of computer art work created by
kids around the world. Check out the art files
from Brazil, Denmark, Israel, the Netherlands,
New Zealand, Russia, Slovenia, Sweden, the
United Kingdom, Uruguay, and the United States.
Submit your own work, too!

### Krannert Art Museum  P

http://www.ncsa.uiuc.edu/General/UIUC/
KrannertArtMuseum/Guide/GuideContents.html

Feast your eyes on twentieth-century art,
medieval art, European and American paintings,
Asian art, near eastern art, and sculpture. You'll
find it all here along with notes about the pieces
and biographical facts about the artists.

### Leonardo da Vinci Museum  P

http://www.leonardo.net/main.html

Meet Leonardo da Vinci, a remarkable Italian
painter, thinker, scientist, and designer who
lived during the Renaissance in the late 1400s and
early 1500s. Check out some of his paintings, such
as the Mona Lisa and the Last Supper, and some
of his radical designs for flying machines — da
Vinci even designed a helicopter way back then!

### Musée du Louvre  HL  P

http://meteora.ucsd.edu/~norman/paris/
Musees/Louvre/

Touch down in Paris, France, and check out the
real Mona Lisa's smile at the Louvre. This museum
holds many of the world's priceless treasures.
Take a look at its collections of Egyptian,
Oriental, Roman, and Greek objets d'art. Then
click your way around "gay Paree"!

### Plugged In Home Page  M  P  S

http://www.pluggedin.org.

These kids are really plugged in. Stop at this site
and check out the stories, drawings, and projects
that kids have created at a state-of-the art multimedia lab in East Palo Alto, California. Plug in
your mouse and your brain!

### World Art Treasures  P

http://sgwww.epfl.ch/BERGER/

Take a good look at the pieces of art at this site.
They're priceless treasures that come from
ancient civilizations and places around the world
such as Egypt, China, Japan, India, and Europe.

## THE "WRITE" STUFF

### Children's Literature Web Guide  HL

http://www.ucalgary.ca/~dkbrown/index.html

Here's an awesome guide to kid lit — literature,
that is — on the Net. Use it to find online stories
and books, kids' writing, and online markets for
your own writing. Get clicking!

### Cool Word of the Day

http://www.dsu.edu/projects/word_of_day/word.
html

It's just so . . . so . . . aeolian! Huh? If you're
looking for interesting words to spice up your
writing or conversation, then you'll want to
cruise by this site often. It features a cool word
every day. Just click on the word to find out what
it means!

### CyberKids  DF  HL

http://www.woodwind.com/mtlake/CyberKids/
CyberKids.html

Click your way through this nifty magazine published by kids for kids on the Net. If you've got a
story idea or some art you'd like to see published
in this e-zine, then Cyberkids wants to hear from
you. It's a great place to find cyberpals, too.

### International Student Newswire  HL

http://www.umassd.edu/SpecialPrograms/ISN/K
idNews.html

Hungry for some news? Park your mouse at this
international news service for students and
teachers and click through news bytes, sports
bytes, feature stories, people stories, how-to stories, and reviews written by kids. Send your own
stories to Newswire, too!

### KidPub

http://en-garde.com/kidpub/intro.html

Get published on the Net! Zoom over to KidPub to
read stories written by kids and to find out how
you can get your own stories published. Write
on!

### MidLink Magazine  HL  P

http://longwood.cs.ucf.edu:80/~MidLink/

This radical e-zine links 10- to 15-year-old kids
around the world. Each cyberissue is crammed
with lots of fun stuff: kids' art, laugh links, the
"write" spot to submit your own writing, virtual
tours, and more.  MidLink also hooks up  to scientific projects where you can ask real scientists
questions. It's a way cool read!

# 3-2-1-Blastoff!

Look on the inside back cover (opposite) to find your **CyberSurfer Cyber Blastoff Disk**. It's jam-packed with neat stuff to make surfing the Net easy and fun. Just open the disk and start clicking around!

Click on the CyberSurfer title wave, and you'll find a copy of the book cover. You'll also see what some people have to say about the book and the disk you're looking at. There are links to sites for **Advanced CyberSurfing**, where you can learn more about the Net and sharpen your Net surfing skills.

Available only on the Cyber Blastoff Disk is your **CyberSurfer Certificate**. Fill in the blanks with information about yourself and your favorite Net activities. If you are online, just point and click to automatically send the information to the CyberSurfer page at OWL Kids Online. In reply, you'll get personalized e-mail to welcome you as an official CyberSurfer. Online or not, you can print your certificate to sign and hang near your computer.

The **CyberSurfer "Yellow Pages" Directory** has been programmed on your Cyber Blastoff Disk in the form of hypertext links. With Internet access and a graphical Web browser, you can just click on the links to instantly get to great sites for kids all over the world. At these sites you'll find information, pictures, sounds, movies, games, stories, cyberpals, projects, answers to thousands of questions, and just plain fun. Plus many sites have **hotlinks** to take you surfing right onto the next wave. The almost 300 sites have been grouped in 25 categories: clicking on the name of a category or on the icon beside it will call up the links and short descriptions of what you'll find at each site. Don't forget to check out the **Cyberstops** — places on the Net where wacky and wonderful things are possible!

A special feature of the Cyber Blastoff Disk is **Hot Stuff**. Here you'll find links to some super downloadable software — FTP programs, e-mail programs, browsers, virus checkers, compression programs, and programs for video, audio, virtual reality, and more.

## What Do I Need?

You need Internet access and a graphical Web browser to use this disk in either Windows or MAC. This disk has been constructed in Netscape 1.1 to be read on a full color monitor. Use of a full color monitor is strongly recommended. The hypertext links will work with a monochrome monitor and any graphical Web browser, but some of the visual and text formatting may not appear exactly as designed. Netscape can operate in any of the following environments at minimum:
**Intel:** Windows 3.1, Windows for Workgroups 3.11, Windows 95, Windows NT; on a 386 or above processor.
**Apple Macintosh:** Macintosh System 7.x, Mac OS; on PowerPC family, 68020, 68030, or 68040.

### System Requirements

|           | Minimum Processor | Disk Space | Minimum RAM |
|-----------|-------------------|------------|-------------|
| Windows   | 386SX             | 1 MB       | 4 MB        |
| Macintosh | 68020             | 2 MB       | 4 MB        |

## What Do I Do?

To use disk:
• Place disk in floppy disk drive.
• In your Web browser, open file BLASTOFF.HTM from the disk.

**Notice to consumers: This book cannot be returned for credit or refund if the disk sleeve is opened or tampered with.**